A GARDEN IN THE HILLS

Weeds... the ever-recurring problem

A GARDEN IN THE HILLS

KATHARINE STEWART

FOREWORD BY

Naomi Mitchison

Illustrated by

Anne Shortreed

MERCAT

www.mercatpress.com

First published in 1995 by Mercat Press
10 Coates Crescent, Edinburgh, EH3 7AL
Reprinted 2006

ISBN-10 1-84183-098-4
ISBN-13 978-1-84183-098-8

Set in Garamond and Benguiat at Mercat Press

Printed and bound in Great Britain by Bell and Bain Ltd

CONTENTS

List of Illustrations   vii
Foreword   ix
In the Beginning . . .   xi

OCTOBER   1

NOVEMBER   6

DECEMBER   15

JANUARY   23

FEBRUARY   35

MARCH   49

APRIL   56

MAY   62

JUNE   72

JULY   85

AUGUST   91

SEPTEMBER   102

ILLUSTRATIONS

'Weeds . . . the ever-recurring problem'   *frontispiece*

'A boletus or two to cook in a little oil'   3

'Down the wooded slope towards the big loch'   12

'A Victorian water-can, bought at a garden sale'   20

'But gardens must rest . . .'   31

'A swarm landed on a sturdy plant'   37

'I look on this old garden with new eyes'   45

'Drawing back the curtain, I looked out'   58

'They will fashion most beautiful wreaths'   66

'A white foxglove stands, tall and straight'   74

'A sleek, dark body scrambles ashore'   82

"You have orchids growing in the yard!"   92

'It will always be June'   108

KATHARINE STEWART lived on a croft at Abriachan, near Loch Ness, for many years. Her experiences during this period of her life are recounted in her classic *A Croft in the Hills*. She has since helped to set up a crofting museum in Abriachan. Now living in Inverness, she recently celebrated her 90th birthday.

Other books by Katharine Stewart include:

A Croft in the Hills
A School in the Hills
The Post in the Hills
Crofts and Crofting
The Crofting Way

FOREWORD

BY
NAOMI MITCHISON

A garden is always pulling one like a three-year old grandchild wanting to get away and do something that the grown-ups don't want him to do. Things you put in carefully just decide not to grow. Or else something you almost throw away produces a flower that takes your breath away with its beauty. What you see from a book may show things as they are in a garden, or it may only show you things that someone—the gardener—chooses to let you see. When you read this book you must decide how real is the picture that goes into your mind's eyes. I think this book will help you to see things as they are, their problems and difficulties, but also the special beauty of a garden in a difficult place, the excitement when everything goes well. In a book like this the happiness, the flowers and the people go on and on for as long as you read it.

Naomi Mitchison

Dedication

To my family, who share my love of gardens and the hills

In the Beginning . . .

God Almighty first planted a Garden. And indeed, it is the purest of Human Pleasures. It is the greatest Refreshment to the Spirits of Man.

Francis Bacon

When the three of us—my husband, my daughter and I—came to live in the old schoolhouse at Abriachan we had just, reluctantly, had to give up working our croft a little further up the hill. Before long, therefore, we had the three quarters of an acre of school garden made into a mini-croft with chickens, a goat and honey bees, as well as many kinds of vegetables and flowers.

It had been hard going, as the ground had been neglected since the closure of the school some years previously. But we worked away, clearing drains, mending fences and dykes. We planted a plum tree to companion the old apple-bearer and brought in fan-tail pigeons to delight the eye. Soon we were able to see a pattern emerging and to relax a little.

My husband was postmaster, working from a tiny office in the front porch, and I was teaching in Inverness. As his health was beginning to fail, though he would never give in, I took early retirement to be at home full time, but sadly, a few years later, he died. By that time, our daughter was married, with a growing family, and living on a farm some twenty miles away.

I carried on the work of the Post Office. Now, left on my own, I found the garden my source of joy. Since that first garden was planted 'east in Eden', so many have blossomed, in so many different ways, and have been at the heart of so many peoples' lives. Thousands of years ago, in Arabia, South America and elsewhere, men scraped over some ground, drove off marauding animals, made a hole with a stick and dibbled in some seed.

Since then we have seen such miracles as the Hanging Gardens of Babylon, Tudor Knot Gardens, Versailles, Sissinghurst, Giverny, Pitmedden, Inverewe, and beloved plots such as the one tended by the mother of Laurie Lee.

To me, my garden has given me the chance to consider many things. For instance, there's the mystery of growth—how that tiny acorn can become that massive oak; that small, brown bulb develop into that dazzling flower. Sometimes I wonder whether this whole planet of ours is capable of growth, of change, of evolution. Of course, I am not a scientist, but science itself now acknowledges, I believe, that there are, perhaps, things it does not fully comprehend.

By recording some of the days spent in and around this garden, I may, I hope, be able to share it with people, unknown to me, who love gardens and the hills and with those, too, who may not have the blessing of a garden of their own.

My friend Anne Shortreed who captured so happily, in line, the spirit of the place, died a few years ago. She came often to see me. She loved the garden and the hills surrounding it. Naomi Mitchison, whose appreciation I cherished, she too, is no longer with us.

But life is here. My daughter and her husband and family, with their combined youth and strength and love of plants, have made a most beautiful garden, full of colour and greenery, out of these beginnings. It will give joy for many years to come.

I should like to thank Tom Johnstone of the Mercat Press for his ever sympathetic handling of the text and I am grateful to Highland Regional Council for permission to quote from the Log Book of Abriachan School.

OCTOBER

October 19th

'The snow-birds are here!' That's a form of neighbourly greeting, the first acknowledged signal that winter has really arrived in these uplands. This year the snow-birds—the fieldfares and redwings—are having a feast, for the rowans are loaded with berries. The old trees at the top of the garden are alive with the flutter of wings and the delighted chatter of hungry birds. A long flight they've had of it from their northern homes and we're glad to make them welcome, reminding ourselves that they're fleeing from winters colder than ours.

The geese came in some weeks ago, and are still coming, some stopping in nearby firths, some making for estuaries further south. It's always thrilling to hear their wild voices and to stand in amazement, staring at the brilliant formation of their flight.

Through the window it's a delight to watch the antics of our own small garden birds—blue-tits, coal-tits, great tits, siskins, chaffinches—as they chase from one nut container to another. A robin looks on angrily, frustrated by his lack of acrobatic skill. A couple of wrens, who sometimes seek shelter in the house, and a tree-creeper or two, along with the blackbirds and thrushes, make up our winter company, now that the summer birds have gone. A flock of long-tailed tits sometimes flits through the garden on its way to the plantation up the road, where the bullfinches dazzle the dark pines.

As everything settles into winter retreat, we miss the company of butterflies and bumble-bees. This has been the year of the butterfly. In early summer the small blue and the Scotch argus came out in the welcome warmth, then white cabbage and tortoiseshell were everywhere, orange-tip on the wayside flowers and, in late September, four red admirals on the marguerites, so unafraid one could have reached out a hand to touch them. One memorable summer, painted ladies appeared among the herbs.

The honey bees are snug now in their winter cluster. Walking up to check the hive, on the well-trodden path through the stand of willowherb which makes their summer paradise, one comes back, covered in white fluff, to tackle the last of the garden harvests—the late potato crop. The shaws are blackened by early frost, but the tubers come up safe and sound, dry and handsome, with a lift of the big garden fork. They're a joy on the plate, as they crumble and melt in the mouth, almost before there's time to savour the taste! The peas and beans have cropped well. Carrots and beetroot gave more meagre returns. The onions are small but well ripened and good keepers. Leeks and turnips are always a great stand-by and are the making of many a pot of broth. The kale crop looks ready to survive the winter through. This year I sowed some extra seed to supply a neighbour whose plants always get decimated by rabbits.

October 23rd

Waking to find a scattering of snow above the tree-line on the hill, I think 'time to gather the apples'. The day turns brilliant blue and gold and wind-less, and just to gaze at the apples—some red, some green, tinged with yellow—against the deep blue of the sky is a moment of delight. They come crisply from their stalks, the ones within reach. A good shake of the higher branches and soon the biggest and brightest are lying on the mossy turf. The old tree—it must be nearly a centenarian—is still putting out new shoots. I think it's a happy old tree. The scholars would scramble over the garden wall, when the master was having his dinner, to pillage the forbid-den fruit. Though it looked so attractive it had a bitter taste, better suited for pies and jelly. The discarded cores must have given many a night-time meal to playground rodents of many kinds.

The plums are not so plentiful this year. The tree must have been hav-ing a year off, though the blossom was beautiful. But wild fruit is everywhere. The rowan berries we make into jelly, a bitter jelly, even when mixed with crab-apple juice, but good as a relish. Our great favourite is rowan wine. We simply steep the berries in boiling water with a small piece of whole ginger, let it stand for ten days, strain, and add sugar, a pound to a pint. Then, after three weeks, or when fermentation has ceased, you have a drink of a colour to delight the eye and which possesses, so they say, the secret of eternal youth. I drink a glass at supper-time each day!

On the wooded slopes down towards the big loch there are brambles, rose-hips, haws, sloes, fruit enough to fill a store-cupboard for the longest winter. And this has been the year of the mushroom, as well as the butterfly. I think the early warmth in May and June, followed by plenty of moisture, may well have done the trick. Fungi are everywhere. I keep to the three I'm sure of—boletus, field white and chanterelle. This year I've tried drying the last two, with some success. At the moment I can gather supper from the roadside—a boletus or two to

a boletus or two to cook in a little oil

cook in a little oil, perhaps with an egg, and a cupful of brambles to eat with a dash of yoghurt or cream.

There are hazel nuts in plenty, too, for protein. They do well in the grinder, then mixed with onion and oatmeal to make 'hazelburgers'. I often think that at this time of 'Oktoberfest' one could survive quite happily on natural produce. Time is needed, of course, to gather in the harvests and to prepare them for keeping, with sugar or vinegar or salt. We're lucky, indeed, to find so much almost on our doorstep, or within easy reach.

October 25th

A glorious blue sky and time for a day off from harvesting and preserving garden or natural produce. So, into the hills above the tree-line, past the russet and gold of larch and birch and, warily, into the domain of the red deer. The stag's roar reminds us to keep our distance, as we watch him through the field-glasses lording it over his placid hinds. The roar is echoed from across the hill, a rival stag appears, and there is the clash of antlers. It's thrilling to watch and hear this annual ritual, which ensures the survival of the fitter hero and so of the fit herd. We stay a while, then retreat, before we're mistaken for possible rivals of another ilk. Homeward bound, we stop at the river to watch for leaping salmon. Sure enough, a huge fish jumps, leaving a widening circular ripple on the smooth, black water. This shatters the reflections of the golden trees, then subsides till another fish emerges. It's good to know that all this roaring and leaping means that another generation of these marvellous species is assured.

On our own territory there's another stop to be made—at the small hill loch up the road. It's mostly covered in thin ice this day, but over by the rushes there are patches of melt and there, upending or sailing majestically, their necks proud and straight, four whooper swans, dazzling white in the dark water, have stopped overnight. Another sure sign of winter, this, but a happy sign. We hope others will come and that they'll stay for a while, keeping company with other winter visitors—goldeneye, goosander, pochard, little grebe, along with tufted duck and mallard.

October 31st

Back to work again! Gertrude Jekyll, I remember from her writings, was a great believer in hard work, so she must lead the way. A walk up the bedraggled garden reveals a massive tidying-up operation is waiting. But the wind's in the east, with scutters of sleety rain numbing the fingers. This is when you long for a greenhouse, preferably a heated one. The small one I bought second-hand some years ago for a few pounds has, alas, not survived the gales. In it tomatoes ripened, along with peppers and even a cucumber or two. But one can make do in other ways. One year a crop of mushrooms appeared mysteriously in some compost in the garden shed. And I've grown marigolds, sweet william and pinks in trays on a sunny bedroom windowsill.

So with thoughts firmly fixed on next year's bounty, I set about gathering burnable dead growth to add to the pile already lying dry under a plastic cover. Dried stalks of willowherb and docken, withered raspberry canes, wind-blown branches of birch, pine and rowan, the garden trees, all make excellent ash to scatter on the strawberry bed. I can almost feel the sweet succulence of the first fruits of next June.

At dusk the bonfire rushes into light, defying cold and sleet, and roaring a welcome to the guisers. In twos and threes they come, in the strangest assortment of garments, some with painted faces shining weirdly in the firelight, some carrying traditional turnip lanterns. A song or poem or a dance for apples and nuts makes a great celebration, as the evil spirits are banished for another year. Better than any firework display is the light of colours—red, yellow, blue, green—in the heart of the fire and the swoop of flame and spark into the black sky. And there's the warmth for numbed fingers and the prospect of tatties baked in the embers later on. Far into the night the glow lingers, till we cover it with earth for fear of a rising wind. Under the ash will be one spot of really weed-free ground, we reflect.

Weeds . . . the ever-recurring problem, that's the one we shall have to get down to again next day. The persisters—docken, sorrel, bishopweed, creeping buttercup—will be carted by the barrow-load to the compost heap. Smaller growth—shepherd's purse, chickweed et al—will be dug in with the lime or organic fertiliser.

NOVEMBER

November 4th

A sudden blast of cold air from the east and hoar-frost transforms the picture from the window. The trees stand motionless in a dazzle of white, as though decked out for Christmas. The grasses are tall still, and strong enough to carry their own small crowns of crystal. And over this whole amazing scene the sky is an arch of deepest blues.

It's a day to be out, to forget indoor chores, to put every available scrap on the bird-table and to don scarves, gloves, thick stockings and balaclavas. The garden ground gives the ring of iron to the spade. There's no chance of digging up a carrot for the soup-pot. It's not even a day for a bonfire. The pile of debris set aside for burning is stiff with rime.

So it's down the road to the woodland while there's warmth in the unclouded sun. Rose-hips are still bright on the bushes, each one capped in white. And the darker red of berries on the old hawthorn glows bright in the wayside hedge. What of the sloes, I wonder, as I turn off to follow the track through the wood. A touch of frost improves most berries, but this freeze-up may be just too hard. The rowan berries were few this year and the meagre crop had gone to beleaguered birds.

The path is slippery with frosted leaves. I search in vain for a few fallen hazelnuts. There will be time to gather them yet. In older times the women would walk barefoot the ten miles to the town, carrying baskets of nuts to sell for Hallowe'en. This is deserted woodland, with its own feel of enchantment and intrigue. Big hazel trees, blown down in gales, lie across the way. This is where a neighbour and his brother used to gather the wood to make superb walking sticks. Delicately tapered, with a curved and polished handle, they are a joy to finger and to use. I treasure mine.

Walking on, stepping over fallen trunks, stooping under branches, I reach the outcrops of rock under the high banks. Here, in little hidden bothies with a camouflage of heather, the illicit brew was distilled. Some was sold to meet the ever-increasing cost of rents. The elixir was renowned. Excisemen would sail up and down the big loch, looking for tell-tale signs of fires, but the distillers knew of a smokeless fuel—the juniper. Bribes were offered for information but to accept would be unthinkable, unless the information were misleading and the money could be used to buy new equipment!

I wander on, taking a short cut down the wooded slope towards the big loch. Enormous oaks grow here, dwarfing the birch and hazel. Druids must surely have found it a place to offer sacrifice, perhaps to teach the young, to heal the sick. It is certain that on the sheltered ground below, where the great burn cascades into the loch, Columba's followers made a settlement when the saint was on a mission to Inverness. His 'font' stone is there, a huge slab of bedrock with a hole in the middle, which, mysteriously, is always filled with water, though there is no apparent source. Within living memory the women would come to give their babies a surreptitious lick of this water, though the minister had baptised them officially in church. There are still signs of early occupation here—marked stones and grave slabs— and a preaching site is recorded in the eighteenth century. The monks were skilled agriculturalists, growing food crops and healing herbs, so it is appropriate that this is where our local Nursery Garden is, on the site of the monks' garden of 1,300 years ago.

The big loch steams when the frost is hard. The water level is strangely low. This has been a sunless summer, but the rainfall can't have been as great as it seemed. Rocks show up stark and black, especially the big one, once used as a look-out post for the steamer coming. Legend has it that it was thrown across the loch by a witch on the other side to avenge a quarrel. As the sun dips behind the hill, I make my way back by the road, refreshed by a foray into what seemed like another age.

When the thaw comes there will be jobs in plenty. Leaves, leaves, leaves are everywhere. We curse the clutter of them in rhones and 'valleys' on the roof, but we're glad to gather them, to make nourishment for generations of growth to come. The trees discard them graciously, leaving branches bare and fragile, outlined in delicate shades of mauve and orange. Some leaves, not twisted by frost or wind, I gather for their shapes and colours— red, yellow, brown. In my hand I have an ivy leaf, dried but still green, pale green, with gold veining. Tall grasses, with rushes from the loch shore, myrtle and heather shoots, all from the moor, dried, bring the beloved outdoors into the house for the winter.

November 8th

A glorious day. Very often we get this bounty in November, an out-of-season day of still-warm sun and brilliant sky. Spring is always late and often disappointing, but autumn makes amends with these bright surprises.

The grass is still green, though the bracken's golden. It's a time to leave spade, rake, hoe and barrow in the shed and take a jaunt up the road. Coming quietly on the loch, round the edge of the trees, we check that the swans are still there. Once, on a day such as this, we chanced on a rare surprise. The air was still, with a touch of frost. The water was calm, yet there was a sound of splashing. We looked back along the tree-lined shore. A family of otters was having a marvellous game together, totally unaware of any intruding eyes. We sat to watch as the heads bobbed, the tails thrashed to the tune of happy grunts and squeaks. Then, as though exhausted, the two adults and the two young quietly submerged and swam away to their resting place among the rushes.

Today there is no sign of otters, but the swans are superb as they come gliding towards us, heads held high on long, straight necks. They seem as tame as the curved-neck swans of picture post-card fame. But, looking at them, we remember the hazardous flight they've made from the ice-floes of the north. Here, they'll gather strength for the flight back in spring to rear their young in the brief arctic summer.

A heron rises laboriously from the small island and flaps his way, with slow wing-beats, into the rushes on the far shore. He knows all the likely spots for a feed.

We make our way back through the pines on the shore. The needles are inches deep underfoot. We gather them in handfuls. Well-rotted as they are, would they make a mulch to keep some of those weeds at bay? Would they be too acid? We'll be back another day with a bag and give it a try.

Reaching the road again we find other treasures that must be fetched. Contractors have been at work gouging out great ditches at either side, revealing layers of peat, quite irresistible for making compost of John Innes type, along with saltless sand the builders have left behind at a housing project. Everywhere there are stones for rockeries or raised beds, most beautiful chunks of rose-red granite and shiny whinstone. Further along are small deposits of abandoned grit and gravel, fine and large, ideal for mulching rock plants or making plantings on scree.

So, planning to return on a real recycling trip another day, we reach home at dusk.

With twigs as kindlers and a couple of logs from the old pine that fell to a gale last winter the fire is soon blazing. And there's toast with a spread of last summer's honey and a huge cup of tea. Thus energised and thinking of the treasures of the roadside, I sit down to write a reasonable letter to the Council asking them, please, not to send the mower up next year to trim the wayside verges. A neighbouring council, I hear, is very progressive in this respect. We hope ours may take heed. The wild flowers must be allowed to come again. The early ones—primrose, wood-sorrel, violets—are safe enough, growing well in from the verge. Those at risk are the summer ones, in particular lady's smock, the cuckoo-flower, beloved of orange-tip and other butterflies.

November 12th

We're back to more normal weather now, with days closing in long before tea-time, skies of several different shades of grey and a hint of sleet in the rain. Soon we shall begin to count the weeks to the shortest day, as if counting had the miraculous power to make the time go more quickly. But no one can tamper with time. It must have its own way.

Meanwhile, the most boring jobs begin to loom. The outhouse across the back yard hasn't been turned out for years. Taking a deep breath, putting on thick boots and gloves and pocketing a torch, I venture in. There is a strange mixture of smells—of damp sacking, perished rubber, turpentine—some quite impossible to identify. I shine a light into the far corners. Some stones have fallen from the wall where ivy has encroached under the eaves. There is broken glass on the cobbled floor. I gather the stones and lay them ready for replacement with cement later on. The ivy has now been cut back. It would gladly rampage everywhere, even through the smallest cracks round the window of a disused room.

Then bags and pails and boxes are filled with broken jars kept for vast jam-making times, discarded bottles meant for summer wines, old paint brushes, worn and petrified, broken hand-tools, rusted and paper-thin, half-empty tins of paint, long since solidified. There is a box of odds and ends of things which might have come in useful—scraps of metal, leather straps, reels of wire. I discard most of them, hoping that there might be a recycling agency somewhere . . . Then it's a great pushing of barrow-loads of the packaged rubbish to a point where it can be taken to the big dump ten miles away. There, I'm thankful to say, it will be placed in appropriate sections for further disposal.

Another day is needed to complete this uninspiring work. Occasionally I come on something with a whiff of nostalgia about it. Wasn't that the hand-fork I used to disentangle the overgrown rockery all those years ago? It has lost its handle and I bought a strong one made in China some time since, so it must go to the graveyard—or, hopefully, the place of resurrection—of half-broken tools. That rusted heugh, hidden in the far corner, as I turn it this way and that it brings back so clearly the days spent hacking a way through the rank growth round the apple trees, when I used to wish for a machete in my Christmas stocking!

9

Cracked plastic flower-pots are the most depressing objects. One imagines them staying in their cracked or broken state for all eternity. Broken clay pots can have a useful further life, providing drainage for future plantings. When at last enough floor space has been cleared for a sweep with the hard broom to reveal the cobbles again, I retreat for a coffee break. Then, grasping the comfort of the warm mug in both hands, I look round at the emerging order. Those floats and a tangled piece of fishing-net brought back from an island holiday years ago bring an instant vision of ice-green water and shining pebbles on a clear white beach. They can't be discarded. I can think of no actual use for them, but they are there, in their own right, themselves.

There are other things like that—parts of a bee-hive, recalling summer days when I had eight colonies busy working the flowers, a Victorian water-can bought at a garden sale, marvellous in operation, but so heavy it sapped one's strength on warm evenings. These are things I shall still give space to, now that the real rubbish is cleared away.

Tea-time brings tiredness, but a sense of relief, a tedious but necessary task having been disposed of. I linger a short while by the fire, then feel impatient for some breaths of air to banish the dust of the debris. Perhaps a short walk up the road? I put on a thick jacket and scarf and step outside. The sky has cleared, cleared to a strange luminosity. I reach the gate and look to the north, beyond the trees. Great shafts of light are moving, fading, re-appearing, across the whole of the northern sky. I turn and look to the west, the south, the east. The whole arc is now lit by moving beams of coloured light, coloured pale green and blue and gold. It's a glory and must be shared. I go in and ring neighbours who might be sitting, unaware, at the fire. Voices and footsteps are heard. 'The lights! Aren't they magnificent?' 'They are!' 'Are the children up? They must see the lights'. No man-made spectacle could come within a mile of this. We wander till the lights begin to fade and the 'merry dancers', as they are called, begin to slow. Then it's in to stoke the fire and to let the wonder sink in. They say it means a change in the weather when the lights are bright. No one can remember ever seeing them as bright as tonight, so what kind of weather will surprise us, we wonder.

There are books and papers to hand and . . . catalogues! A catalogue of flowers, not vegetables but summer flowers; that's reading that will match the mood, I decide. Just to look at them is real delight, now that colour photography has reached such perfection. Hollyhocks—this year I must get some hollyhocks to grow against the wall at the back of the border. Pyrethrum, delphinium, canterbury bells, all my favourite flowers are here. I turn page after page, then go slowly up to bed to drift into a marvellous sleep, with the lights still reflected on the ceiling.

November 20th

Thoughts of summer may make many a happy evening dream, but reality comes in the morning, with tales of six cars stuck on the hill road, in an early frost that caught the gritters unawares. And then—snow. So work in the garden has to be minimal.

The first snowfall makes it possible to check what marauders may be up there among the winter greens—the kale and broccoli and spinach. Sure enough, the unmistakable pattern of the hare's footprints is there, also signs that the local pheasant has been on his rounds. Later in the winter even leek-tips will be eaten by the very hungry. Luckily, I'm spared the ravages of the rabbit, though some years ago I had to resort to desperate measures, covering each cabbage plant with a plastic pot to keep it safe. Neighbours not far away still have the problem, now that myxomatosis seems to have disappeared. In older times, roe-deer must have been a menace, as there are vestiges of a stretch of wire-netting above the four-foot wall. But I have only once seen a roe here, when a hind appeared outside the window, quietly grazing on the green. Keeping well hidden, I watched her move off and leap gracefully over the wall and into the scatter of pines on the hill beyond.

What I would dearly like as a garden resident is a hedgehog. I have tried. One evening, walking home at dusk, I spotted a small creature ambling quietly up the road ahead. I couldn't believe it—a hedgehog! He seemed to be waiting to be picked up in the newspaper I happened to be carrying! I managed to open the door with one hand and groped about for a big cardboard box. In this, with a saucerful of cat-food, my hedgehog spent a peaceful night. Next morning I carried the box up to the top of the garden, laid it on its side, open to the wilderness, with another saucerful of food nearby. But I never saw my lodger again.

Another time, in October, a neighbour brought me a hedgehog he had found on a road miles away. A box again and a dish of cat-food and, as it was near hibernating time, I put him in a deep bed of straw in the shed. But, sadly, he did not survive. I'm still hoping one small, trusting, prickly creature may yet come up the garden path, like what he finds and stay around.

November 25th

This is Thanksgiving Day in America, thanksgiving for the early immigrants' first harvest. The Canadians celebrate theirs more than a month earlier, on October 11th. There are probably many reasons for this—climatic, social,

Down the wooded slope
towards the big loch

possibly religious. But I wonder whether the fact that so many of the early Canadian settlers were of Scottish highland origin has anything to do with it. Certainly those that survived the horrors of the voyage out must have been hardy and resilient. Some were, of course, bitter at having to leave their homeland, some were ambitious and eager to make a new life. They were all used to tackling hard physical tasks and to enduring days of numbing cold and near starvation. They could also savour a time of achievement. Their first harvest home must have been a great thing to celebrate.

I see them, at least in their early state, when they were prospering well enough in their original homeland, as our first conservationists. Alexander Carmichael, in his book *Carmina Gadelica*, a collection of traditional Celtic lore, tells us:

> A young man was consecrated before he went out to hunt. Oil was put on his head, a bow was placed in his hand and he was required to stand with bare feet on the bare grassless ground. Many conditions were imposed on the young man, which he was required to observe throughout life. He was not to take life wantonly. He was not to kill a bird sitting, nor a beast lying down, and he was not to kill the mother of a brood, nor the mother of a suckling. It was at all times permissible and laudable to destroy certain clearly defined birds and beasts of prey and evil reptiles, with their young.

In the 'Hunting Blessing' there are these lines:

> Thou shalt not eat fallen fish or fallen flesh,
> Nor one bird that thy hand shall not bring down,
> Be thou thankful for the one,
> Though nine should be swimming.

Hunting was not a sport then, but a means of surviving, for the hunter and the hunted. Simple rules kept greed and impetuosity at bay. The people were always aware that there was a power in the world far greater than themselves. It was a power which could be invoked for blessing on every aspect of their lives. So from the rekindling of the fire in the morning to the smooring of the fire at night there was a blessing asked for every one of the day's activities—milking, herding, sowing, reaping, clipping, weaving, fishing, rowing—everything, they felt, would prosper if blessed. Perhaps it was this sense of working along with the powers-that-be that helped them to win through, even in the most adverse conditions, in their new homes in the New World.

My own Thanksgiving Day would have been somewhere between the Canadian and the American one this year. One day about the middle of October I could have gloated a little as I made the first really big pot of autumn broth with leeks, onions, carrots, swede, beans, parsley and sage, all home grown, with a little imported barley for bulk, followed by a panful of tatties cooked till they crumble, eaten with a pat of butter and cheese, and apple and bramble purée, made from the few apples my old tree produced this year and a chance picking of scarce brambles made on an outing to a favoured spot.

That was a memorable meal and it has been repeated many times, with a different pudding, perhaps one made with the strawberries my neighbour kindly kept for me in her freezer. She also kept for me, last year, some cowslip seed, as I was told it liked to be frozen. I duly planted it in a pot of compost when the time came and waited. The waiting was long. Now, at last, I see some tiny plants, recognisable as minute cowslips, are emerging. I'm leaving them to face some more cold and hope that, in spring, they'll really grow. They're very scarce in these parts. I've seen them flower in only one place—the railway embankment on the route south. Railway embankments do host many lovely plants. This one sports marguerites, corn marigolds, flax, comfrey and many more. They must have been there since the days of steam and soot.

I'm told that plants are thriving along the big motorways now, along with wildlife of various kinds. This sounds like some sort of a pact between man and nature. The nearest main road here is certainly no motorway, but it's bordered with flowers from April to October—primroses, daffodils in masses, then foxglove and marguerites, with honeysuckle climbing the trees, wild roses and woodland strawberries on the banks and, of course, all the heathers in season. In autumn, the trees put on their own display.

Wildlife mostly keeps its distance, for it has plenty of other living space, but roe deer and hedgehog do venture onto the tarmac and get killed. Pine marten and foxes are tempted by the picnickers' remains.

Thinking of these things helps to get the shortest days on their way. Daylight from 7.30 in the morning to 4 in the afternoon is little enough when the chores seem to take longer each day. Clearing snow, sweeping leaves and twigs after a gale, gathering kindling, fetching coal, arranging the unavoidable shopping trip, all these things take up energy and time which one longs to spend creatively. But nature has a time of hibernation. We must give in graciously and take to keeping warm and replete.

DECEMBER

December 1st

To celebrate the first day of the last month of the year the 'power' is off. Machinery of all kinds has to have its days for overhaul and replacing spare parts. We know that and are forewarned, though sometimes we wonder why it has to be done in times of gale, frost, snow, whatever the winter may be throwing at us.

For those of us who remember pre-power days the loss of the 'electric' for a day or two is not a great hardship. Sometimes I think of the Tilley lamp with a whiff of nostalgia. Once it was primed and pumped it made such a comforting hiss and gave a real feeling of warmth, as well as shedding soft light on table, book or bed. Candles were always at the ready, as they are today. I'm up sharp this morning, in balaclava and woollen coat, to get the fire going and to set a kettle on the picnic stove.

At other times we are left in the dark without warning, though experience has taught us to anticipate trouble when the gale is from the north-west or the snow is lying heavy on trees and cables. I remember the time when the power-line was being set up. How the men accomplished it, in weather of every kind, is a story of heroic proportions. Erecting giant poles in remotest moorland, climbing them to fix the cables, ferrying in material—I'll never know how they managed to achieve these feats of skill and endurance. Several times we had a worker in to thaw out frozen fingers and to down a hot drink.

When the power was finally installed the celebrations were legendary. The only drawback was that once an elderly neighbour had acquired an electric heater for her kitchen there was no smoke signal from her chimney in the morning to let us know she was up and well.

One funny story went the rounds. A grandfather who wasn't going to bother putting in the electric at his time of life, went to stay for a few days at his son's home, as was his wont, to recuperate after flu. His son's wife put on the heater to warm up his room and the lamp beside his bed. In the morning he was up early. 'How are you today, granda?' he was asked. 'Ach, I was wakened a' night . . . The candle's in a bottle and ye canna' blaw it oot!'

The men who are called out these days to repair the power lines on black nights of snow and gale are as heroic as their predecessors who set them up. We really have little to grumble about as we sit up late beside a glowing fire, reading by the light of the candle we can 'blaw oot' if we wish.

Listening to the wind in the trees and to the sound of driven snow battering the window panes is a great refreshment to the spirit, making one realise, as our ancestors did, that there are forces we shall never control, that we must learn to live with them. A little humility is quite comforting.

Of course, there are problems for people with lives dominated by technology. Deprived of power, machinery breaks down. Freezers and fridges disgorge their uneatable contents, the T.V. screen is blank, the telephone dumb. Clothes must be washed by hand, as long as the water runs free. Tropical fish may perish in their tanks. There's also the question of transport. With side-roads sheeted in ice and the main road blocked by drifting snow, cars sit aimlessly in yards or garages. I'm glad I can go happily on foot to visit neighbours within my radius. I'm glad, too, that I have never lost the habit of stocking the cupboard in early winter with oatmeal, flour, lentils, tea, coffee, sugar, dried milk and tins of beans and peas. My back kitchen is as good as a freezer when the wind's in the north, so that cheese and margarine keep the length of several storms. I do the cooking wearing mitts and balaclava!

This is when you re-discover the pleasure of listening to the radio. Mine is battery-operated and portable so that it's always on hand for listening to news bulletins and weather forecasts. On candle-lit evenings it's quite a treat to tune in to great music, a poetry reading, a play or, perhaps, a repeat of one of those marvellous old comedy series 'The Goon Show' or 'Round the Horne'.

I'm glad to hear that radio is being re-discovered anyway, storms or no storm. It's a medium which spurs creativity, as reading does, when images spring alive in the listener's mind.

Being snow-bound for a spell, cut off from the busier world that one is aware of out there, humming with activity, can certainly be a blessing, giving pause, a healthy pause. Should something unforeseen occur—a serious illness or accident—then recourse could be had to technology of a life-giving kind—a radio help-call link summoning the services of snow-plough, ambulance, or, should conditions allow, helicopter. We need never feel forsaken.

December 15th

More early snow today and a very heavy fall, the branches of pines and cypresses weighed down alarmingly. The school mini-bus couldn't cope with conditions on the hill, so the four-wheel drivers got into action, ferrying children and messages. Phone-lines are intact, but soon the electric power goes off, when a tree collapses onto an installation several miles away.

Fire-glow and candle-light are better than anything the 'electric' can provide, after a day coping with frost and snow-drifts. But cooking on a spirit-stove is limited in scope. This year, however, a kind neighbour who has a solid-fuel cooker provided the most wonderful surprise—a hot meal brought by torchlight and on foot!

With the thaw came branches brought down by the weight of wet snow, a slate or two off the roof and rhones displaced, the usual battle-scars. Nothing could be done in the garden, of course, but my thought was for the bees. Normally, I don't feed them till after new year, but the summer had not been a good one for honey and they might well be short. I made up a feed of icing-sugar, mixed with hot water to the consistency of putty. This they love. On lifting the lid of the hive I found a mouse, or mice, had been having a happy time, nesting in the warm covers and no doubt feasting on honey. I slipped my offering on to the top of the brood-frames and for my reward got a very painful sting on the eyelid. At least this meant the bees were alive and kicking! I tidied up the mess and went back for a trap for the marauders.

The snow was melting fast. Pausing near the door, blinking from my sting, I noticed a small winter marvel—buds, tight-curled, on the white lilac near the door. With this reassurance giving a lift to the whole day, it's in to the fire again, curtains drawn against darkness and cold, to dream up gardens of the mind.

Here's one! Through an archway of yellow roses there's a stretch of grass, herbaceous plants flanking it, in curves of glorious colour. Further on, to the right, along a stone-flagged path, herbs grow, in shapely plots. Then there are the rows of vegetables, tidy in season, the soft fruits and the old trees of apple and plum and beyond these again, the corner of a wilderness, where the bees suck willowherb and thyme and there's a small stone seat under the rowan. Not that there's anyone sitting there, least of all one's self, for sitting is a rare pastime in a garden, even an imagined one. On those few afternoons when it's too hot, shall we say, for weeding, in the garden of reality, it's usually a question, not of sitting, but of stretching out on the grass, face well covered in midge lotion, gazing at the bloom on the little cherry tree and the blue arch of the sky above and breathing in the scent of honeysuckle and clover. But there are many short strolls to be taken, shutting one's eyes to weeds and faded flower-heads and revelling only in the living shapes and colours. I always reckon it's summer when I can carry breakfast tea and toast out to the garden, sip and crunch by the hawthorn hedge and throw crumbs to the fledgling blackbirds. The wait for mornings such as those seems interminable. But gardens must rest. That's what this one is doing now. Roots are snug, well below the reach of frost. Above ground there's the dazzle of frozen grasses and the delicate outlines of bare bush and tree. And, as I bend to look closely, there, under the window, is the first thrust of hellebore, the Christmas rose, the flower itself resting on the bare ground. It's almost incredible how anything can work its way up through the cold earth, to the winter light, in these short days. But then a garden is an incredible, living thing. And it's an integral part of the house that it surrounds. Coming in from a short winter walk to the welcome shelter of the old rooms you find signs of the garden everywhere. By the window there's the potted geranium, brought in to bide its time till spring. From a bowl of dried herbs on the table the scent of summer rises. You stretch your fingers to the fire and watch the flames curl round that bit of birch you had to cut from the old tree after the autumn gales. A cup of tea—and you wonder—raspberry jam or heather honey on the toast? Both are familiars of the garden. Everything is known.

While roots are resting and light hours are short, then is the time to think about the actual garden, as well as those of the mind, to think, to plan and to remember. Remembering, first, means an outreach beyond the scope of present memory to things recorded more than a century ago. This garden is roughly a quarter of an acre, carved from a heather slope. The house sits squarely facing south, fronted by flat ground. Behind it there is a gentle rise, to the contour of the hill and the protection of a four-foot wall of natural stone. The window makes a good hide to watch whatever may appear—a red squirrel in the ivy, rabbits and hares sitting up on the grass to wash behind their ears, the cock pheasant abandoning his stately gait to try desperately to balance on the bird table, siskins and great tits doing gymnastics on the bags of nuts hanging just beyond the glass and birds of many kinds in their season. Butterflies and moths, too, fly close by in fearless animation.

All this, and more, was here over a hundred years ago, when the site was levelled for the building of a school and schoolhouse. The first master to live here, Mr Maclean, must have had a job wrestling with the natural ground. Even today the wild growth takes every chance to reappear. Clumps of heather and rushes will surface among the tattie drills, clover swarms into the strawberry bed and willowherb makes a protective curtain around the bee-hives. As long as it's kept in place, it's more than welcome there as a valued source of nectar and a most attractive backdrop to some rather stolid rows of neeps and kale.

Successive schoolmasters must have done what they could. In the Inspector's Report of 22nd February 1909, when Mr Campbell was in charge, it is stated that 'For the further development of the Nature Study, Practical School Gardening is to be introduced forthwith.' And so it was, by April 9th.

On June 20th 1912 we read that 'The Garden was inspected by Andrew T Fowlie of the College of Agriculture.' There were problems. On May 11th 1923 the entry records 'As sheep are constantly breaking into the garden work has been stopped till the walls are rendered sheep-proof.' I know exactly what he meant. More than sixty years later the sheep, the more agile variety, are still sometimes managing to leap over the wall, where the superimposed netting has given way. That can mean goodbye to all the summer lettuce and the winter greens, not to mention the precious flowering plants and all the work that went into producing them.

On 7th November of that same year the Log Book records that 'The school garden has unfortunately had to be placed in the lowest grade as, for want of a fence, the plants and vegetables were devoured by sheep.' Some ten years later, on June 14th 1934, 'The school was visited by a Mr Black, organiser of agriculture for the county. He gave a lesson on agriculture in Scotland, crops and stock, and inspected the school garden.' His verdict is not recorded.

At the end of the following year Mr Neil, the teacher, retired and Mr Denoon, a keen gardener, was appointed. In October 1936 the Log Book records that 'The garden here is in course of reconstruction. Plans have been carefully made and the results are looked forward to with great interest and confidence.'

The Inspector's Report for 1937 to 1938 records 'The Head Master and his pupils deserve great credit for the improvement effected in the layout of the school garden. The results in the horticultural side enhance considerably the amenities of the school.'

On June 30th 1938 'Colonel Baillie (of Dochfour) visited the School, signed the registers and had a look round the school buildings and garden. He is giving a prize for the best kept plot and is sending his gardener to examine said plots after the summer vacation with a view to judging the best.' This was encouragement indeed. The next Inspector's Report (16th August 1938) records that 'The Head Master here has transformed a poor, neglected garden into something very pleasing and deserves very great credit. With the help of the pupils the following improvements have been carried out: flower plots, herbaceous border, lawn, rockery, crazy paving, hedges, rustic fence with roses, all carefully planned and neatly executed. The productive side is also included and the educational aspect kept in view.'

a Victorian water-can,
bought at a garden sale

During the war, as part of the 'dig for victory' campaign, the lawn was made into a potato patch. In 1941 lectures were given on bee-keeping and by the following year there were hives to be inspected in the garden. Mr Denoon also kept chickens and goats in a bid for self-sufficiency. In close on ten years he had created what was almost a smallholding and a very attractive one. But the school roll had fallen to 45 and thereafter was to decrease steadily until, in 1958, only two small girls remained and the school was forced to close. Subsequently several short-term tenants of the school-house came and went, so not much was done to the garden. When we arrived, wild raspberries, willowherb and sweet cicely had largely taken over. To bees and butterflies and to many kinds of birds, this was paradise! For us, it held all the thrill of uncharted territory. Every day a fresh discovery was made. Even now, I come on surprises each summer.

As the top growth was cut down the outlines of the old plots began to emerge, terraced to follow the upward slope of the ground. We borrowed a rotavator and decided to clear half the area the first year. When digging began we came on stone drains. The cost in work hours involved in laying them must have been tremendous. Realising how essential they were we tried to protect them, though subsequent work has, unfortunately, caused damage in places.

Digging revealed many other interesting things—worn-out toys, pieces of pottery, a pile of school slates from a dump against the top wall, evi-dently discarded when jotters came in—and, most interesting of all, several 'scrapers' dating from prehistoric times. An archaeologist friend told us some years ago that the garden was plainly on the site of a bronze or iron age settlement. Just over one wall is a hut-circle which we long to have excavated some day. Meanwhile, I often imagine my predecessors here look-ing on the same outline of hills, the same scoop of the burn in the hollow, listening to the same sounds of lark and owl, the bark of deer and many more long gone—the howl of wolf, maybe the growl of bear. The heather would have been their late summer delight, making drinks of tea or ale, thatching for their roofs and kindling for their fires. Sometimes I envy them the simplicity of their lives, though the hardships must have been great. They didn't have a Christmas to celebrate, but they knew all about the winter solstice and they must have been happy to see the bright berries on the holly, as we do today.

Christmas preparations here still hold the magic of earlier times. The holly and the ivy grow just outside the door. The tree is a small spruce with roots which I dig up every year from the garden and replant later. It thrives on this treatment and each Christmas sports a slight fresh green top shoot.

Welcome neighbourly home-produced gifts circulate—shortbread, honey, eggs, hand-painted cards, wax candles, plants and the most beautiful arrangements of dried flowers. Brightly wrapped packets of tea for pensioners are handed in, with a greeting and a smile, by members of the Community Council. The local school makes up hampers for a few lucky senior citizens. And the children practise their carols in preparation for their evening round, even remembering those favoured by different households.

After Christmas there's the ceilidh, with much music—clarsach, accordion, fiddle and pipes—and song and dance. And, with the past not having quite caught up with us, we have the bonus of keeping Christmas going till Twelfth Night and the date of 'old' Christmas!

JANUARY

January 2nd

The diary is silent on the first day of the year. Good resolutions are buzzing in the head, along with memories of new years long gone and of the one just celebrated. In older times the head of the house would open the door to let the old year out and the new year in, then he would step outside to fire a shot at any evil spirits that might be lurking about. Shots from other places would be echoing. Then, armed with a bottle and a lump of peat for luck, it was time to set off to first-foot the nearest neighbour.

Nowadays we meet in the house of our oldest neighbour for Hogmanay, drink a toast as midnight strikes and then it's singing, in Gaelic by our host and by some of us trying valiantly to follow, in English by others, and a dram by the glowing fire for each succeeding visitor, till the room is so warm that pullovers are discarded and tea is made to revive flagging energies. Neighbours who may not meet often, leading very separate lives these days, each having their sphere of work, cherish this chance to meet and engage in communal enjoyment. The intimacy of shared song is very special, as eyes and smiles meet, each voice with its own pitch and intonation, carrying the singer's memories and meanings. Parting is reluctant, even in the early hours. But home means a deep and dreamless sleep, more refreshing than longer time spent in a half-waking state.

Day-time visitors arrive as the black bun comes out and there's still a half-bottle of something in the cupboard. This is a day when people largely dependent on motorised transport—car, quad-bike, tractor, van—find their legs again and go walking, with children running, not strapped to car seats, and dogs let off the lead when the sheep are safely by-passed. Summer plans are discussed on long walks up the forestry roads, plans for garden development, for summer holidays, for sorting out the ever-growing accumulation of books and papers, so that chairs are uncluttered and visitors can take their ease! Thoughts of the shed clearance are inspiring. Perhaps Oxfam could benefit. One and every project seems possible of achievement as the new year swings in.

With the light fading and when the day's visitors have gone I feel a sudden hunger for a good bowl of freshly-made soup, to chase away the taste of rich, sweet cake and wine. In the vegetable rack are carrots, onions, turnip, the 'keepers' of the harvest. Taking the small fork I go out into the

23

dusk to prise up some leeks. The ground does not resist. There is even a feel of freshness about it, as though it might be turning in its winter sleep, at the touch of the new year. There is parsley, lemon-scented thyme, balm and sage in the sheltered containers by the window. I add barley and a few lentils and soon a great potful of broth is simmering happily on the stove.

Later, sipping my bowlful, with a big heel of brown bread, I think of that bare, brown ground outside and resolve to make a start at forking in the compost next morning, while the going looks good.

Sure enough, in the morning the going is good and, to my amazement, as I step outside, I'm greeted by the sound of birds giving voice, softly, happily, in the hawthorn hedge. I stop in my tracks to listen. Was I mistaken? No, I hear them again. Could this be my reward for feeding them regularly through the hungry days? It must be the slightest increase in the length of daylight, which they, with their hyper-sensitivity, can detect. If the people in high places had sensitivity to match that of the natural world our lives might be better lived.

I put out more seeds and nuts and a ball of fat to keep our song-birds in good heart and voice and plunge the big fork into the compost-heap. There's plenty of good nourishment there. I spread barrow-loads on the bare ground for next spring's salad crop. A flight of long-tailed tits flutters by overhead. They are too shy to come to the bird-table, but they seem fit and lively on whatever sustenance they can find.

January 12th

With the 'new' New Year well and truly brought in, we remember that today is the day of the 'old' New Year. An elderly neighbour used to say that by this date there was 'an hour on the day'. Sure enough there is the feeling that this old planet may just be tilting its face towards the sun. As I watch the great dazzling winter orb travel slowly along the ridge of hill opposite my window it seems to me it disappears just a little further to the west. The tree-covered slope below is in its winter glory. The Forestry Commission wisely left the 'natural generation' untouched. Now there are wedges of dark green conifer between the stands of birch—skeletal and mauve—with a border of russet larch. The colours are incredible. I've asked an artist friend to paint it for me.

On this 'old' New Year's day the second snowfall of the winter keeps us from work outside, but watching the whirling flakes and the ever-lengthening icicles along the eaves you remember the blessings of winter. Roots will be lying snug under the insulating cover and the frost will be killing off unwelcome pests. Siskins venture out of cover to join the tits at the nuts hanging by the widow. Fox and pine marten risk daylight robbery in a neighbour's poultry run. All life has a hunger to be satisfied.

That night the wind moans out of the north-west and by morning the whole world has changed shape. Trees are bowed down, the tips of their branches touching the ground. The boundaries of field and road have disappeared under great mounds of snow. Everywhere there are sculpted patterns of indescribable beauty.

By noon the wind slackens and we have to get out. The usual signs of garden visitor are there—the tracks of hare and mouse, bird-prints, too. We can't grudge anything to any creature on such a day. All that protrude are the tips of giant kale. There's a deep pile of snow on the roof of the hive, but that will keep the bees cosy. Then it's a walk up the road, kicking steps all the way, looking at the blue light in the hole made by the stick, marvelling at the snow-shapes and watching as their contours slowly change with the guiding pressure of the wind. It's a living landscape. We're in, we feel, at the fashioning of a new world.

With the early fading light the wind falls away, the sky clears to reveal a dazzling sunset. The frost will be a killer. Of course, we don't grow tender plants up here—we're 700 feet up—and everything is well acclimatised. My worry is the water-pipes! One year the pipe carrying water from the spring far up in the hills froze outside. I had to resort to breaking the ice on a nearby burn and filling pails. This went on for nearly a week, with much time and energy consumption. Now I have bales of hay, covered in plastic, at strategic points outside and lagging of many kinds, including old nylons, inside. So, it's in to the fire and a routine check of lagging. Then—supper. There's leek and carrot soup to hand for a warm starter. Then the oven goes on to heat up the kitchen and I slip in two big tatties in their coats, a big onion and a huge apple, stuffed with honey and sultanas. And I'll wash that down with a glass of rowan wine!

I often think we miss a lot by ignoring or discarding the natural growth that surrounds us. The original hill folk of this upland area had the reputation of enjoying long and active lives. Nowadays incomers have deepfreezes and easy access to the supermarkets in the town. How their health and strength and longevity will compare with that of their predecessors has yet to be seen. But the wild plants are there, in their hundreds, to be had for the picking and choosing, fresh in spring and summer and preserved dried, pickled or fermented—for autumn and winter.

We're lucky enough to miss out on chemical spraying. The little fields have gone, mostly, to sheep grazing, the foresters are wary of our drinking springs and those of us with gardens grow organically. So . . . to the hills, the background of all our lives. Hills mean heather and heather is food for sheep, deer, hares, grouse, all the life of the hills, and for many insects and honey bees.

In older times it had many uses besides—for thatching, rope-making, the making of baskets, brooms and scrubbers and for bedding and fuel. For humans, the flowers were used as a brew—a hot infusion or an ale. In the far ancient times the Picts made a drink of young shoots of heather, mixed with thistle and honey. The invading Romans were said to be envious of the strength of their Pictish enemy and to have tried, in vain, to discover the recipe for the drink that seemed to give them almost miraculous power. Nearer our own day, Robert Burns is said to have enjoyed heather tea, made by infusing three or four sprigs of dried flower heads to a pint of water. Robert Louis Stevenson had a poem on heather ale:

> From the bonny bells of heather
> They brewed a drink lang syne
> Was sweeter far than honey
> Was stronger far than wine.

Now, down from the hills and to the garden—and the weeds. But what is a weed? The Oxford English Dictionary says it is 'A wild herb springing where it is not wanted.' But mine are not unwanted, not totally. The butterflies and bees would agree. Mine include nettles, docken, bishopweed, thistles, willowherb, chickweed, sorrel, dandelion, silverweed, tansy and many more, a rich source of vitamins and minerals. Feverfew and sweet cicely thrive like weeds and have to be continually cut back and plantlings given away to friends and neighbours. Taking each one:

Nettles:
It is said they were introduced into Britain by the Romans, who couldn't live without them! They are full of iron. Pick them young, wearing gloves! Cut them down later on for a second growth. Cook them like spinach or make them into a delicious soup, with a little onion and a thickening of milk, with butter and flour or oatmeal. They can also be made into wine or beer. They make a valuable addition to the compost heap and I have a friend who rubs them on rheumaticky knees to relieve pain! In older times the fibres were used to make cloth and dyes.

Docken:
Unlikely as it seems, these can be stuffed, as the Greeks stuff vine leaves. Use young leaves and stuff them with rice, onion, egg, herbs.

Bishopweed:
This was probably also introduced by the Romans and once cultivated as a

pot herb. It was said to be good for gout and was grown at inns and mon-asteries. It can be cooked like spinach.

Willowherb:
The young shoots can be used as a substitute for asparagus! Cook the leaves fresh as a green vegetable or use them dried as a herbal tea.

Chickweed:
This plant is rich in iron and copper. It was once sold in bunches, like watercress, at markets. Use it like cress in sandwiches or in salads, plus the flowers. It also makes a delicious cream of chickweed soup.

Dandelion:
A beloved plant which brightens the spring of the year and delights the bees. Use the young leaves in salads or in soup. The flowers make wine or tea (four tablespoonsful to a pint of water). The roots, cleaned, dried, ground and roasted make an excellent substitute for coffee.

Sorrel:
This is a plant, a member of the docken family, which loves my damp, acid ground. It is much prized in France. The leaves give a sharp, lemon flavour to salads and the soup is really superb. Take 1 lb. sorrel leaves, 4 oz. butter, 4 cloves of garlic, 2 pints of water, 2 oz. of flour, $^1/_2$ pint of cream, salt and pepper. Enjoy it chilled in summer or hot in winter.

Silverweed:
Known as 'one of the seven breads of the Gael'. It was cultivated at one time in the highlands and much used before the introduction of the potato. The root was ground into flour for baking.

Going beyond the garden walls again and taking a summer or an autumn walk along the hill tracks or down the path into the wood bordering the big loch (Loch Ness) we find, and we smell, three aromatic herbs. First, wild thyme growing in the short turf, wild mint among the grasses and wild garlic in the damp hollows by the burn. The mauve-blue flowers of the thyme, when dried, make a drink on a winter day that brings all summer back. Mint and garlic I use sparingly to give savour to soup or vegetables. Wild comfrey grows here, too. The dried leaves make a healthy infusion (2 teaspoonfuls to a pint) and, soaked, they produce a valuable fertiliser, being full of potash. In older times the root was grated and used as a plaster, whence the old name for the plant 'bone-setter'.

Meandering, now, up the road to the little loch on a summer's day, a swim in the cool water in mind, we come on the summer flowers which I asked the council verge-cutter to avoid. We use them, of course, very sparingly and only when they are flowering in profusion as these three do:

Meadowsweet:
An infusion of the flowers is an excellent cure for headaches, the dried leaves are good for flavouring and, of course, there is the sparkling 'champagne'.

Lady's Bedstraw:
The flowers make a honey-flavoured tea.

Clover:
Both red and white make a pleasant infusion.

Near the water's edge, among the dwarf alder and willow, there are stands of wild raspberries for refreshment and on the moor ground, further on, are blaeberries to stain the mouth and fingers and to take home for pies and jellies. Later, there will be mountain cranberries to gather for sauce.

Autumn is, of course, the real harvest time. That's when a walk down through the wild woods of oak, hazel, birch, rowan and pine that fringe the big loch will reap rewards. First, we come on the roadside rose bushes with their clusters of shiny red hips, so lovely just to look at and full of vitamin C. A little further down there are hedges of blackthorn with the berries just coming to their purple bloom. Very bitter they are, but good for a winter drink and, of course, to add to a bottle of gin. The rowan berries glisten in the sun, a glorious sight when the sky above is blue. They make a good, slightly bitter jelly and, of course, a very acceptable wine. Juniper grows in some profusion in the clearings. At one time the berries were exported from the area to Holland, for the making of gin. Nowadays they are used to flavour boiled potatoes or cabbage and they do add a piquancy to many dishes. There are elderberries, too, for wine, and haws, but the most succulent crop is the bramble one. Some bushes grow with their feet right in the shallows of the loch and when we've gathered them and tasted them, to our delight, we can walk over the beautiful, rounded pebbles on the shore and wonder what creatures may be living under the water. At a winter tea-time spreading the jelly on a scone, all the feel of the autumn gathering-day comes back to mind.

Retracing our steps and keeping our eyes on the ground we find hazelnuts. Sadly, there are fewer squirrels nowadays, so this means plenty of nuts among the fallen leaves. They are said to contain more protein, fat and carbohydrate than eggs. They can be roasted, salted, and put into the blender with a little butter, to make a nutritious spread, or, of course, they can be eaten raw, as can the other ground-cover we come on in the moss among the birches—chanterelles. They are a delight to look at, with their delicate, fluted, saffron-coloured underlay, and to smell, with their apricot scent, and to taste. Better still, cook them gently in butter when you get home. Then there are boletus, which make excellent soup, white field-mushrooms, puff balls and many more. They can be dried or frozen and made into memorable winter meals.

We who have access to all these natural foods in a relatively pollution-free area, are, of course, the lucky ones. Friends from central Europe, over on holiday, were amazed at what we neglect or despise. Boris, from the Czech Republic, would come home from a walk up the nearest hill with a rucksack bulging with dead wood for the late summer fire and a hatful of berries and, to me, unidentifiable fungi, most of which I wouldn't dare to eat on my own but which he would turn into an unforgettable supper dish—which we all survived!

Here are four possible menus:

Spring
Nettle soup   *Rowan Wine*
Mushroom omelette
Salad (dandelion, chickweed, willowherb shoots)
Raspberry compote
Dandelion coffee or herbal tea

Summer
Sorrel soup (hot or cold)   *Dandelion Wine*
Stuffed dockens
Ground elder (hot) or salad
Strawberries and cream *or*
Blaeberries and cream
Dandelion coffee or herbal tea

Autumn
Mushroom soup   *Meadowsweet Wine*
Hazelnut purée on toast (with rowan jelly)
Brambles and cream
Dandelion coffee or herbal tea

Winter

Potato soup   *Elderberry Wine*
Hazelnut roast (with rowan jelly)
Dandelion roots (stewed)
Blaeberry pie
Dandelion coffee or herbal tea

January 18th

A winter aconite, flowering through the snow! True, it's in a sheltered spot, close by the front door, but its flowering seems a miracle, nevertheless. I take a close look at the small bed under the window. Sure enough, the Christmas rose is not to be outdone. The darling bud is lying there, tight closed, on the white ground, ready to open when the cold eases.

This is not the weather for garden work, apart from checking fences, but in the short, bright afternoons there's time to walk and look and plan. Every year I try to take in another small piece of overgrown ground, a little patch to be sown to kale or sorrel, something for the winter soup-pot or the spring salad. This is a garden on the wild side, and the wild would so soon take over. There's still plenty of wilderness round the edges, where wildlife is more than welcome, but the plots must be harnessed, not allowed to bolt. This year I plan to clear what looks like a most unpromising few square yards in the lee of a leggy hedge of cotoneaster and where the roots of willow and rowan lie. Rhubarb, given by a neighbour years ago when we first brought the garden back into cultivation, planted with a good dressing of dung, is doing well nearby and apple mint is thriving. So I reckon a good pile of manure and compost should make this small piece of desert bloom, once the weeds are out. We're lucky in having supplies of manure to hand—farmyard stuff just up the road and horse dung down the way. These do bring in weed seeds, particularly chickweed, but a handful of that is delicious, eaten like cress in a tea-break sandwich, and the rest goes onto the compost.

I must have one of the biggest compost heaps in the country. In fact, I have three or four, but I'm afraid I don't organise them methodically. Some of them sprout a variety of weeds. Spectacular nettles for the butterflies are allowed to thrive and subsequently put back in again. From time to time I excavate the bottom layer and dig out loads of good black loam from well below the reach of noxious seeds or roots.

Over the years I've learned to live with my weeds. For some I've even acquired a degree of tolerance. Nettles do make that delicious soup and

But gardens must rest.....

bishopweed (ground elder) really does eat like spinach. My most persistent and invasive plant (I don't want to call it a weed) is sweet cicely. I think it must have been introduced at one time as a useful herb. Certainly the flower can be used as a sweetener when stewing rhubarb or other tart fruit. And there's the clerical connection, too. I believe the monks, in former times, used it to make liqueur. I wish I had the recipe! It rampages here. I used to try to dig it up, but the roots grow impossibly deep. Children use the stems as aniseed-flavoured pea-shooters. I give small plantlets to friends, with dire warnings about keeping it in check.

Another plant which appears regularly in spring is feverfew. I lifted one some years ago from the abandoned garden of a former croft house up the road. The mistress there, I was told, 'grew many herbs'. I think she must have been one of the lost generation who knew what herbs could do. I now give plants of feverfew to friends who suffer from migraine and they consider it beneficial. A few leaves eaten straight from the plant do bring relief. And the small, daisy-like flowers are very attractive.

Dandelions I allow to flourish, even in the strawberry bed, as they are an early attraction to bees, butterflies and other insect life. I even planted two rows of them, near the hives.

The main delight for the bees, of course, in later summer, is the willow-herb. It is allowed to form a great swathe, almost engulfing the hives. One year, a swarm landed on a sturdy plant, bowing it almost to the ground. That was one swarm easily collected and put back safely in a hive.

Another bee crop which I planted some years ago is clover. I cleared a patch not far from the hives, bought good agricultural seed and sowed it. Now, it is rampant! But it's easily shifted where it's invasive and it nourishes the ground. It has taken over the grassy paths between the plots. Walking there is almost like walking on a chamomile lawn!

The one weed I do heartily dislike, which has put in an appearance only over the last two years, is the horse-tail. This really unpleasant-looking little 'soldier' is the bane of my life, as it marches on, invading a little more territory each year. And it has perniciously inextricable roots! It's not a plant I'd care to talk to. The language might become unseemly. I can imagine, though, having quite pleasant conversations with the willowherb, if I could make myself heard above the buzzing of the bees!

January 25th

'As the day lengthens, the cold strengthens'. These old sayings invariably ring true. Something has happened, lately, to the direction of our wind-flow. The prevailing westerlies, reasonably mild and bringing welcome soft rain, have been swinging to the north and even to the north-east or south-east. One day I'd like to consult a meteorologist. We, whose lives are so closely linked to weather conditions, really need such a consultation, as we sometimes need one with a medical doctor. The television weathermen rarely get their suns, clouds and arrows quite right for our particular area. Sometimes I feel like shouting back at them when they, somewhat smugly, predict mild air for us and wintry conditions further south, when we are lying under six inches of snow and goodness what is happening in the Pennines!

Wearing clothes almost too heavy for active service I step out into the cold. The snow has gone for the time being, but the ground is sodden. Great heavy clumps stand up in weird shapes, sculpted by the frost. Leaves and shoots of winter greens have been chewed off by hungry hares. Branches and twigs lie in unusual places, scattered by those alien gales. The compost heaps have been ravaged. Undigested scraps of kitchen waste—tea-bags, egg-shells, onion skins—clutter the path. It's a scene of desolation. Will anything ever grow again? I have to remind myself that roots and seeds are lying snug, below the reach of frost, or warmly blanketed by snow.

There will be time yet to doctor that leached earth, to scatter compost and a sweetening of lime. I think of the islands in spring, when the winter gales have driven the white shell sand onto the coastal grass and this precious ground, the machair, is suddenly a carpet of flowers.

I can expect no such miracle, of course, but nevertheless, in a sheltered corner, near the west wall, I come on a tiny primula, blooming quietly to itself. That atom of reassurance is enough to make the day. And the day is lengthening now, by a good hour. I wander round, checking the bee-hive for signs of marauding mice, piling fallen branches, raking leaves, till the light fades at five o'clock.

Indoor chores become unbearably tedious when one is impatient to get on the move outside. I remember a farmer friend who kept Sunday as a day of rest, yet couldn't bring himself to sit at the fire, but would be out roaming the fields, planning the season's work, looking over the sheep. If he dropped in to a neighbour's house the talk would be always of the weather, then the state of the crops and beasts, before a grumble or two about the government, national or local. There's never a question of boredom when it's a struggle to survive. The weather can be a common enemy or blessing. Every morning means a step into the unknown, the largely unpredictable.

Feeling as restless as our farmer friend, I go in to make a phone call to another farmer, one who lives nearby. Could I get a load of manure, please, perhaps while the ground is hard, so that the trailer won't stick. He agrees, quite happily. The byres are needing a good muck-out. I remember how

crofting neighbours used to have strong doubts about the 'artificials', pro-
moted by the agriculturalists all those years ago. Long gone are the days
when the house thatch, well impregnated with peat-reek, would be ploughed
into the fields, along with the saturated straw, bracken or other bedding
material from stable or byre. In the islands, of course, seaweed gave great
fertility. 'Artificials' may produce quick results, on a big scale, but in the
long term the earth needs to be cherished, not force-fed. As long as human
greed dictates policy we shall have those obscene mountains and lakes we
all know about, and an increasingly impoverished earth. Thinking of these
things I get out the box of seed-tags and clean them, ready for this year's
labelling. One small positive gesture can dispel a cloud of doubt.

In the evening, sitting at the fire, I eat supper of mashed neeps and
tatties, with a mealy pudding (haggis is not for me) and drink a small toast
to Rabbie. He had a kinship with animals and flowers, with the whole earth,
which so many have lost. His 'Red, red rose' is surely the greatest love song
of all time.

FEBRUARY

February 1st

This is the festival of St Bride. Her name is the christianised version of the name of the Celtic goddess of spring—Brighid, the modern equivalent being Bridget. The time of Brighid was a celebration of the first signs of returning light and life after the darkest of the winter was past; a time of creative impulse and energy.

Bride of Kildare was an Irish saint who founded a nunnery in Ireland and was the patron saint of many people, including milkmaids. I gave her name to my white Sanaan goat, she of the golden eyes and the elegant, capering legs. She came into milk about the time of Bride's day, giving always an adequate supply, on a diet largely composed of natural herbage.

This year Bride's day dawns unbelievably bright. A step outside and there's the sweet smell of fresh earth. You draw in great gulps of air, scrutinising the sky. Is it too bright, too early? Streaks of pink cloud are stretching from the east, round towards the south-east. The west is faintly blue. Or is it grey? No, it's bluish. That's a good portent, for the weather is in thrall to the west.

I take an early walk round the edges of the garden. Buds are swelling on the flowering currant. Catkins on the willow are beginning to shine. Finches are chattering in the hawthorn hedge. High overhead a pair of buzzards is circling happily. Life everywhere is bursting to emerge.

I go in reluctantly for a quick breakfast, standing at the window, keeping a weather eye on this special day. It still looks promising. The light from the east is golden now as the sun climbs confidently into a clear sky. To the west the blue is deeper. This looks like a superb Candlemas eve . . .

The phone rings.

'It looks like a good day. What about a walk this afternoon?'

'The very thing.'

'Good. See you at the road-end about one.'

There is never any doubt about which road-end is meant. We can take our pick of walks from this particular spot—along the peat-road onto the hill above the tree-line, where the old peat-workings are filled with water now; down the old 'funeral road', the way that was used to carry the coffins shoulder-high to the horse-drawn hearse waiting at the foot, or along the track to the old crofting settlement where only one house still stands.

This is surely one of the most superb walks in all of the Highlands. Originally a footpath, it was engineered by succeeding generations of crofters into a track now navigable by tractors and vehicles with four-wheel drive. Mercifully not many of these use it, so that it's a haven for horse-riders and walkers. Over the edging of conifer and birch there is a wide view to the hills beyond the big loch. The big loch itself lies there below, so near that you can count the ripples on the surface, yet as remote as ever. Along the road the green verges are studded with flowers in spring and summer—primroses, tiny violets, wind-flowers, saxifrage, tormentil—and in the turf down the middle the wild thyme grows. In autumn there are berries—raspberries, juniper and mountain cranberry.

Half an hour of leisurely walking takes us to the house. Tucked into the shelter of a dip in the ground, it's a substantial $1^1/2$ storey structure of the type built about the turn of the century, with a roomy steading—byre, barn and stable. The old single storey house remains, used as extra accommodation for hens and stores. Bits of the old timbers and partitioning can still be seen, though the thatch has long since disappeared. This place, we are told, is one of the few which were not discovered when Cumberland's men were harrying the glens after Culloden. My companion is an artist and has been painting the remaining old houses of the neighbourhood. I'm hoping this one will be her next.

At one time, perhaps 150 years ago, there were five crofts here, five houses, five families. One field is still known as the 'Tailor's Park'—park denoting a field of grass. Perhaps he kept a number of sheep, his wife would spin, he would weave and then make up the cloth. This was surely a sensible procedure, when the town with its tailors was a good day's journey away and they would be charging hefty prices.

There were several shoemakers in the area, too, some practising their trade to within living memory. With the one surname being widely held, people were often known by the name of their occupation or the place where they lived. Thus Elizabeth Fraser became Lizzy Balbeg, Mary Fraser became Mary Tailor if her father plied this trade, William Fraser might become Willy Balagreusaichan if he was a shoemaker.

We linger a while about the house, imagining, sadly, how full of life it must have been at one time: long summer days of work, winter evenings of ceilidh when neighbours would be made so gladly welcome and might be snow-bound for days. The last member of the family struggled on here on her own, with her cattle and sheep, some hens and her devoted collies, till ill-health forced her to leave. The blackcurrant bushes in the old garden still bear quite luscious fruit.

We wander on, then sit for a while on the moss-covered rocks by the waterfall. The little fields sloping down to the trees above the loch are still

a swarm landed on a sturdy plant

unbelievably green. Sheep are grazing contentedly. I spend a moment wishing someone would press a time-switch to take me back to this day, say, a hundred years ago. I could see one man spreading dung, another making a start at the ploughing. A boy would be herding cattle up the hill. I could hear him whistling for sheer joy at being out on this bright day. I could hear children playing by the door, a woman calling, dogs barking. A thin plume of blue smoke is rising straight up from the chimney. There is the welcoming smell of peat. I wake reluctantly from my daydream. The sky is still almost cloudless, only puffs of dazzling white gliding slowly in from the west, like ships in a heavenly regatta. There's a hint of warmth in the sun. It really is a magic day!

I can understand how people living in these idyllic places, living at a measured pace, dependent on things beyond their control—gale, snow, flood—could well imagine that there were creatures around which were also beyond their control, beyond their ken. A man from these parts, who became a minister of the church and served abroad as an army chaplain, told me not long ago that, as a young boy sent to herd the cattle in a green place not far below the house, he encountered a small group of 'fairy folk'. He took the cattle home and went excitedly to tell his mother what he had seen. She promptly gave him a skelping for telling lies. He firmly believed, for the rest of his days, in what he had seen.

About the same time, in another place, an old couple had 'brownies' living in their outhouse. Every evening they would put a dish of milk out in a hollow stone for their small guests. Every morning it was gone and they were well pleased, for the brownies had to be looked after if they were to be helpful.

In the island of Gigha a local brownie who was a most useful helper in the big house—bringing in peats for the fire, washing the dishes and so on—had a pew to himself in the parish church.

Until quite recently the people of the crofts often brought up orphan children along with their own. Fostering had been widely practised in the old days. The chief's son would often be reared in quite humble homes, thus forging the link between members of the clan. I was thinking of these orphans as we walked back along the track. To the children of the crofts every tree and boulder, every corrie and burn was familiar and most often a source of delight. To a child straight from the streets of a city, as most of the 'boarded-out' orphans were, it must have been a terrifying experience to walk this way to school, especially in the winter. I remember once meeting a little fellow on the road, his face a white mask of fear. He had got himself completely lost. I set him on his way. He went on, looking back only once. A few months later I met this same boy with his pals. A wide, cheery grin of recognition lit up his weather-beaten face. His footsteps were sure and confident. Some sort of magic was working on him. He'll be back, as so many like him have been, in later years, to look up his old haunts and his guardians, or their families, and to tell his own children how it all was.

We reach home as the light is beginning to fade. Tea at the fire rounds off this lovely Bride's day to perfection. Bride herself would have enjoyed it, I feel sure.

February 2nd

> Candlemas day, gin thou be fair
> The hauf o' winter's to come and mair.
> Candlemas day, gin thou be foul
> The warst o' winter's ower at Youl.

An elderly neighbour of mine used to quote that to me every year. He firmly believed the dictum and it did, indeed, very often tell the truth.

The very name of the month—February—seems to have connotations of new beginnings, almost of growth, as the hours of daylight continue to increase. Then we remember that other saying about the cold strengthening. It has many germs of truth, too. So we study our Candlemas day with the utmost care.

This year it looks like being just as glorious a day as yesterday. There is the same lift in the air, the same feeling of time stealing a march on spring. I'm out early again to check on wind and sky. There's no movement of cloud, just a clear expanse of pale blue, waiting for the old sun to rise to his full height and suffuse everything in his kingdom below with light and colour. So we accept this day as another godsend, but warily, remembering that old sayings have come down through the generations, accumulating layers of truth.

Chores completed as quickly as conscience allows, I emerge for another check on the weather. There's still no sign of a change. The bees are out, the birds are chattering, there's even a small dance of midges in a sheltered corner of the green. This is a day for positive action. That pile of good-sized stones, which has been growing over the years, has the makings of a rock garden, there, at the turn of the big border. Alpine strawberries are growing there happily already. A patch of wild plants that flourish among rocks would be ideal! I survey the area, then look at the stones again. Many bring back memories of summer expeditions here and there—a piece of white Skye marble, green shiny rock from a north-east beach, sturdy, wave-smoothed stones from the west, whinstone and rose-red granite from the garden itself. Thyme and saxifrage and some little yellow rock-roses would nestle quite contentedly among these stones, I reckon, settling to the task.

The day wheels on overhead. I warm, literally, to the work, oblivious of everything but the placing, and spacing, of the stones. The garden robin keeps me company, flitting from bush to tree, to wall, alighting sometimes on the next stone to be moved, as though signalling encouragement and approval. When hunger drives me in for a bite and sup I suddenly realise that the day is passing, has almost passed, with no drop of rain, no blast of wind. It is fading, now, gracefully, into shades of pale gold, pale pink, with a hint of green where the sun is sinking. So we shall have to brace ourselves for the 'hauf o' winter to come, and mair'. The stones look well. It has been a good day, come what may.

February 6th

The snowdrop month came in with much chirping of finches, 'sawing' of great tits and general commotion among the budding branches of rowan and birch. The blackbird had been singing his 'inward' song for several weeks and was tuning up for his full-throated version to come. Fresh snowdrops were opening daily and a blue primula was venturing into flower in the shelter of the ivy-covered wall. There was warmth enough for the bees to fly down looking for their beloved crocuses. They were not disappointed. They seem to favour the yellows. To see them walking into the opened flower, in a dazzle of sunlight, makes it seem summer's happening tomorrow. Of course, experience tells us otherwise, but we cling to the illusion for a few magic hours. Discarding jackets and with sleeves rolled well above the elbow, we tackle even the most laborious garden jobs with gusto. Collecting dead grass, branches and raspberry canes for a spring bonfire, digging the plot left unturned in the autumn, any job is a pleasure when the first whiff of warming earth is rising.

When friends arrive out of the blue I spread a rug on the short, dry grass and entertain them out of doors. To go inside would be unthinkable. It's a day for the first picnic of the year. Soup and sandwiches, taken under a sky of speedwell blue, in the company of singing birds and happy bees, taste better than any imagined caviar and champagne. We know this cannot last. There are gales to come and blizzards and floods. But a February day of sun and calm makes the most memorable *entr'acte* in the drama of winter.

Sure enough, within twenty-four hours our capricious weather system brings cloud and a west wind with an edge to it. A good time for work in the lee of the west wall, tidying, weeding among the plants in the rock garden. Dead leaves, twigs, even branches are everywhere. It's the penalty paid for having so many trees around. We're glad enough of the shelter they provide, but the debris is great. Rhones and gutters everywhere have to be continually cleared. But at least there is ample provision for bonfires and an endless supply of leaf mould. Weeding at this time of year is not a hard chore. Even the old perennials are easily dragged out, though there's the occasional 'snap' as a stem is severed and I have to probe deeper for the last of the root. The compost heaps grow higher and higher. Straightening up between emptying loads I look up the length and breadth of the garden, imagining how it might be altered. The trees planted for shelter have grown leggy. I have had one or two cut down, one or two have crashed in gales, more will have to go. They take up a lot of moisture and cast too much shade. I spend my rest-pause in contemplation. Will my dream-garden ever materialise? I go back to the job in hand. Soon it will be the time of garden openings. That's a happy thought, though seeing other gardens sometimes makes one despair of one's own!

We're lucky enough to have several nursery gardens within reasonable reach of us here. My favourite is the one I can walk down to, taking a short cut through the old oaks and hazels, right down to the shore of Loch Ness. There, among the rock and heather, the rowan and birch, these neighbours have created a garden of tremendous character and charm. Overworked words, perhaps, but ringing absolutely true in this case. The amount of energy that must have gone into the making of terraces, paths, plots, can only be guessed at. The result is sheer joy. You walk up into the wood, go round a bend and there is a planting of rhododendron, azalea, among the wild growth of primrose and dwarf willow. It's ideal territory for rock plants. They spread and cascade, obviously happy to be where they are. There's a place for everything herbaceous as well. Shelter from the north wind and from the prevailing westerlies makes it an early place. Only occasionally does a vicious easterly come whipping across the loch, and then not at a time to blacken blossom.

February 14th

My valentine arrives in the form of a burst of song from the top of the tallest cypress opposite the window. The blackbird! His practising is over. It's now the full-throated song. I stand absolutely still, gazing up, fearful of disturbing the singing. I can see the movement of his throat as the notes emerge. It's a moment of magic. I know, of course, that it's not a question of artistry, but a challenge he's uttering, a challenge to any others of his tribe who may feel like contesting his right to this particular territory. I back him to the hilt, for he is my particular blackbird.

I remember others—the one who fed his first brood so competently with scraps scattered on the grass, while his mate was brooding their second lot. One wintered in the byre years ago and would sing his quiet, inward song whenever the milk started to spurt into the pail.

This morning the singing is confident and clear, a kind of signal that, from his vantage point, all's well. Then, suddenly, the singer takes flight, straight as an arrow, towards the plantation up the road. He has to be about his business. I shall be hearing him again at dusk.

Meanwhile, I stay a moment gazing up at the empty tree. It's a huge, solid structure, taken so much for granted because looked upon every day, yet really worthy of wonder. That great trunk, tapering as it rises, the strong, supple branches and the delicate fronds, the colossal roots hugging the ground, all this has grown from a minute brown seed. In growing, the tree has scattered further seed, at random, so that saplings can be given to neighbours desperate for shelter for their plants.

I look beyond the garden wall, across the fields to the planting on the opposite hill. Larch, birch and pine make the most beautiful winter patterning of colour, which I never tire of admiring. Will it be allowed to remain beautiful for at least a little while? I hardly dare to hope so when so much is changing hands, being altered or destroyed. I have an artist friend who prefers to paint these trees in winter, when the structure and colour of stems and branch is clearly apparent, without the distraction of leaves.

What of the rain forests? Only now, as destruction goes on, are we beginning to realise what is being lost—people, wild creatures, plants. And the forests of India? Their loss means soil erosion, villages emptied, people starving for the sake of making fine furniture for the houses of the rich. Isn't this absurd?

In our own country it has taken us a long time to accept what our forebears knew generations ago—that native plants, including trees, may provide cures for even the worst of human afflictions. The bark of the willow, long known to contain healing powers, is now being studied as a possible cure for cancer. The willow is said to have been sacred to the Moon goddess. Thousands of years ago arrow-heads, shaped after the leaf-pattern of the willow leaf, were found in burial places. Sallow, or salley as in Yeats's poem, was another name for the tree:

Down by the salley gardens my love and I did meet

Then, at parting, we would 'wear the green willow', one for the other. The old craft of basket-making, still practised today, depended on the small osier willows growing by the burn. The bees get their first cargoes of pollen from the pussy-willow flowers. I turn away to walk up the garden, for a look at my own willow-tree. There is the sound of bees! They can't be sensing nectar yet. No, they're having a cleansing flight and making for a row of white washing on the line! I don't grudge it to them as a staging-post. It's good to see them lively and celebrating a fine day!

I wander on and come to my rowans. The rowan is an amazing tree. I've seen one growing out of a tiny crevice in a rock-face, flourishing quite happily. It's a tree with magic properties. I had a neighbour not long since, who would never burn wood from a fallen rowan on her fire, though she would use it outside to heat food for her hens. Every house had a rowan by the door and a small branch would be fixed over the lintel of the byre and the stable to ensure protection for the beasts against evil. The berries, too, had magic in them and were used in divination rites. Still today children make rowan-berry necklaces which remain attractive even when dried out. Sometimes I have hidden a tin of berries in the ground and dug them up at Christmas to decorate the house. They certainly make a wonderful wine, with a touch of magic in it, and a good red jelly. They can also provide a sweetener, I'm told, suitable for diabetics. The brown and grey bark of my rowan is covered in lichen, so that the limbs look more grey than brown. This lichen means, of course, that the air is pure, for lichen cannot survive where there is much air pollution. Fingering it gently I give a small signal of thanks that 'my lines are set in pleasant places'.

Over the west wall of the garden I look onto an area of heather, moss and natural tree growth. At one time this was part of the common grazing but, as sheep are kept now mostly in fields which no longer grow crops and are fed, in winter, on silage or concentrates, the grazings are abandoned as such and are planted with trees or 'developed' for housing. I climb the wall and look, while I still may, at the self-sown silver birches. Along with the rowan, the birch is one of the hardiest of trees. Its graceful outline, the shine of the bark and the delicate colour of its bare winter branches and of its leaves in spring and autumn, make it a refreshment to the eyes and the spirit at any time of year. Babies' cradles were made of birch and the sap is extracted to make a potent wine.

Dwarf alder grow among the birches on this stretch of moor. The wood of the alder has the unusual property of turning black and hard when submerged in water and was therefore used in the building of bridges and the making of containers for liquid such as milk. The green wood was used to make whistles and pipes. The leaves can soothe burns. Most people rush to find a docken leaf to soothe a nettle-sting. I wonder if anyone looks for an alder leaf to apply to a burn.

Next, in my tree-walk, I come to the hazel. In Celtic legend the nuts of the hazel tree contained all knowledge. It was said that the salmon in the pool ate the nuts that fell from the hazel and so became the 'salmon of wisdom', having eaten the 'hazel nuts of knowledge'. To divine water the hazel-twig was always considered the most appropriate.

I wander on, thinking of all these magical properties of trees and beasts and wishing we still relied on them, for they would tie up many of the loose ends of our lives today. They must surely have helped our forebears to make sense of the world about them. They were surely more worthy of belief by humanity than the stories conveyed by those tottering little figures on the video screen.

The mosses underfoot make wedges of carpet between the heather clumps. They are marvellous plants, growing in soft, smooth hummocks of greenery, some sporting little bright red and yellow flowers, perfectly adapted to their environment, keeping low below the wind, thriving on the peaty damp. A friend who lives not far away has inherited the old knowledge about mosses and lichens, making wonderful dyes for her hand-spun wool. People come out from town, sometimes, to cut swathes of the sphagnum moss. This is probably for flower arrangements, but the moss has antiseptic properties and was widely used in dressings during wars.

Coming back by the road to the garden I pass the hawthorn hedge. It has grown tall and thick and gnarled. Bulky lorry-loads sometimes take a swathe off it when passing by. It's a good shelter from that cold south wind and a welcome roosting-place for many small birds. Its thorns are a good deterrent to erring sheep. On the lower ground hedges such as these were torn out and replaced by fences. What wire fence can give shelter, protection and a tasty bite to grazing animals? The tasty bite is good for humans too. On many a summer walk I've pulled a handful of fresh green leaves and chewed on them for my 'bread and cheese'. An infusion of the berries is said to be helpful in problems of blood pressure, high or low. Everywhere about us plants are there, ready to make us healthy: maybe not wealthy, but hopefully a little wiser than before.

February 18th

Showers of sleet today and a wind rising to gale force 8 or 9. The longing for a greenhouse is strong. But I water the trays of seedlings on the bed-

I look on this old garden with new eyes

room window-sill and visualise the hoped-for result. The bedroom mari-golds did well last year and the sweet william should flower this summer. The dianthus have made healthy growth as edging everywhere.

As the sleet begins to whirl in horizontal patterns and the wind howls among the slates, I tire of watching the tree's precarious bending, turn from the window and pick up a gardening magazine sent by a friend. It makes fascinating reading, but its world seems totally unreal. Asparagus beds, pagodas, outdoor peppers and tomatoes . . . would any of these sur-vive in a hill-top garden, in a climate full of wild uncertainty?

I suppose some of them would, with adequate shelter and sources of labour. Certainly there have been gardens in Scotland, and in the higher reaches of the country, for many hundreds of years. I think of the Queen Mother's garden at the Castle of Mey in Caithness. You can't get a place more exposed than that. Mary, our Queen, had a tiny garden made for her on the island in the Lake of Menteith, where she played as a child for a short while, before being sent to France in 1548.

There was a famous Physic Garden in Edinburgh, originally at Holyrood House, from 1670. James Sutherland had 'care of the garden' and later became 'professor of Bottany in the Collidge of Edinburgh'.

John Reid, gardener to Mackenzie of Rosehaugh in Ross-shire, wrote a book *The Scots Gard'ner*, first published in 1683. It went through several editions at the time, reappeared in 1907 and again in a reprint in 1987. In the preface he says 'because the many books on gard'ning are for other countries and other climates, and many things in them more speculative than practical, this ensuing treatise the rather be acceptable'. He was clearly a gardener for us today. Scots gardeners are, of course, renowned practi-cally the world over. Even to children they are famous, since the appearance in Beatrix Potter's tale of Mr. McGregor.

Perhaps the most famous Highland garden is the one at Inverewe, on the northwest coast, where the Gulf Stream brings a whiff of tropical air, allowing some exotic plants to grow happily. There are many native species, too, and a good feeling of wildness persists. Gerard Manley Hopkins, in his poem 'Inversnaid', says:

> What would the world be, once bereft
> Of wet and of wildness? Let them be left,
> Oh let them be left, wildness and wet;
> Long live the weeds and the wilderness yet.

That poem has given me comfort many a time, when I contemplate my own patch!

February 24th

Persistent cold winds, driving flurries of snow, mean that outside work is held up, though the lengthening days tempt everyone to get on with it. I can remember late February days like the one we experienced earlier this month, so mild that the midges were dancing. Coming down the garden in late afternoon, sleeves rolled high above the elbows, you stopped to watch a lark swing into the sky above the trees, scattering his song, and there, beyond the big loch, the hills had put on their Italianate air, mauve shadows filling the hollows. To the north the high tops still held a glisten of snow, but that might well be there till mid-summer or beyond. It's good to have the mind stocked with memories like these, as good has having a library, shelves well filled with books and documents which can be consulted at will, when you're coping with the present or planning for the future.

This particular day, jacket sleeves well fastened and a scarf tied round the ears, I walk up to one of the wild corners of the garden. Here, more than a dozen years ago, when clearing a patch for planting, I had built some turf sods into a wall to give shelter to young plants. This wall still stands, firmer than ever, welded together with tough grass roots.

I often think of how the little houses of the Highlands were built in prehistoric times. Low walls of stone, traces of which can still be seen just beyond the garden, had long roofs of heather thatch, supported on poles and tapered to a central pitch, in the manner of an American Indian tepee. Later the walls were built of sods and raised higher, the roof supports sunk into the ground. Later still, and to well within living memory, the walls of stone were doubled, with an infill of rubble for greater warmth. In the islands the ends of the houses were rounded to defeat the wind, and the roofs were low and battened down with hanging stones. Hens roosted on the rafters; cows and horses found shelter under the same roof, at a slightly lower level, in an adjoining part of the structure. Humans and animals shared body heats quite happily. These living units were ecologically quite perfect, built with renewable resources, made to fit the environment of hill, glen or shore and adapted to prevailing weather conditions—gale, rain, snow.

Many times I've dreamt of retreating to a small, a really small, fairly remote house, with chickens and a garden patch, with a nearby well, a peat fire and an oil lamp or two. To have no frozen pipes, no electric meter ticking away, no thought of road conditions—would that be paradise? As long as a neighbour's light would wink out at dusk, there was the sound of children calling, a dog barking now and then.

These are late winter dreams, when far horizons always loom! Soon we'll be back in port again, with more practical thoughts!

MARCH

March 2nd

Waking to what looks, from the window, like a reasonable day, reminding myself that this really is March and we should be heading for spring, I hurry through a watered-down version of essential indoor jobs and make for the garden. I work it on what are, I hope, essentially 'green' principles. Scanning it today I smile ruefully as I look in vain for a rewarding sign of anything green. Dead growth I leave on the perennials as protection against frost. This growth now lies in sodden brown masses, covering the entire border and the path. Drifts of wet fallen leaves lie on ground cleared of crops in the autumn. The bare grey branches of rowan and bird-cherry overhang the prostrate brown stalks of the willowherb.

This is the time when, every year, I wonder if I'll ever get things to grow again in any sort of order, yet, somehow, it is achieved. Once or twice I've had the idea I'd like to put part of the garden to 'fostering'. This came about when, some years ago, a young man who had no garden asked if he could use the greenhouse here to grow on some plants. I said 'with pleasure' and supplied him with putty to replace some missing glass. But it didn't happen. He left the place soon after. However, I'm glad to say he then became a gardener and I hope is gardening still.

I very much hope, too, that some of the young people who live here now may get the gardening fever. It has to be a fever, I think, and an incurable one at that, a passion, a lifelong passion, that not even a wheelchair can dampen. The thing must start early in life. I'm always thankful I used to try handling a hoe when I could only just stagger after my father on his way to the vegetable plot. Children today have so many after-school ploys and distractions and maybe haven't the patience to wait for seeds to sprout, though they do grow cress on the windowsill.

I survey the whole depressingly brown scene again. There is one sign of life—the mole-hills in the grass. These I have no objection to. They supply beautiful earth for potting up plants, or can simply be dispersed with a blow of the spade. Moles do sometimes disturb seedlings, but they also aerate and drain the ground. My only fear is that too many of them may destroy too many worms, those much-prized underground workers. So highly valued is the contribution worms make to the conditioning of the soil that they are actually being farmed these days.

Perhaps I really should do something to reduce the area under crop, I reflect. Perhaps sow one plot to mustard or field lupins? They are said to make excellent green manure when dug in in the autumn. Then, weed control really should be tackled. Old carpets are the answer, I believe. I do have some stacked away in the loft, probably making nests for mice. In the garden they smother weeds at birth and eventually rot down to build humus. They can be covered with peat or chipped bark to avoid visual offence. These are things I really should try. Perhaps . . . next year?

A vicious little wind is rising, flinging small, icy darts of rain against my face. It's not such a good day after all. With a shiver in my shoulders I turn away from thoughts of next year. Here and now I must try to warm up at least one small plot, one bed for salad things. The means are to hand, in the shed—tattered strips of black plastic bin-liners, kept from last year. I stretch them out, weighing them down with sturdy stones. If they warm the ground only a little perhaps the lettuces, radishes, spring onions will get away a little quicker than the weeds. I'll soak the seeds, split them, scarify them, do anything that will let them avoid being smothered by that all-pervasive chickweed and its companions.

The rain really has an edge to it now, coming almost horizontally, in wind-chilled bursts. My morning thoughts and hopes of spring are dashed. Of course, our seasons don't go by the calendar, but by whatever is brewing somewhere up about Siberia. I have to acknowledge this was a false start. There will be more to come. Still, I've made a gesture, just a small one, to boost the warming-up process we all depend on.

I retreat reluctantly indoors, make a cup of tea and sip it in the kitchen. My kitchen is the despair of family and friends, most of them. Some are discouraged from even entering. There's a cooker and a sink and a small larder, the usual kitchen equipment. In actual fact this is the engine-room of recycling activities. In every corner, on every shelf, there are plastic containers of all sizes for seed-growing, plastic food-wrappers for making mini-greenhouses, plastic bottles ready for decapitation as cloches for fragile plants. These are at least some beneficial uses to which plastic can be put and I'm grateful for them.

On impulse, I fill a margarine container from a bag of seed compost, which has also found its way into the kitchen, and push in some parsley seeds. Maybe it's just another, devious way to steal a march on spring!

March 7th

At last a day of calm, when to get up and go straight outside is sheer indulgence. There's the smell of earth crumbling from the frost. The blackbird's song is so loud it's almost a call, as he hits one particularly high note. I whistle him back my nearest imitation, which he seems to enjoy. He's perched on the topmost branch of the cypress. We pursue our duet for a minute or two, then, looking down, I stop in my tracks to wonder at the first primrose to flower. It must be spring, though officially it's still two weeks away.

What to do first is the only problem. A neighbour arrives to give a hand at gathering material for the bonfire. Loading and carting goes so much more easily and quickly with two. Everything has been well dried by a day of east wind, so the burning will be easy. One schoolmaster of old had great faith in the value of wood ash, when 'artificials' were almost unheard of. He would get the scholars to collect branches from the wood and great fires would rage for days. Mine is a more modest affair, but the result will be invaluable. At one time a kind neighbour who burned only wood and peat on his domestic hearth used to bring me pailfuls of ash for the strawberries.

When the fire is safely smouldering I make a start at clearing the big border. Dead growth is mostly left till spring as protection against frost. Now it comes away in chunks and goes straight to the burning. Soon it will be time to divide up blue geranium, lupins, marguerites, which quickly overgrow in the shelter of the west wall. Even my most precious astrantia, given to me by a friend years ago, spreads happily. It's good to be able to share these plants with people starting gardens from scratch. Scratch it really is, up here. The first year must be spent digging up heather, rushes, all the moorland scrub, before applying a good dose of lime. Black plastic is spread and at last some sort of tilth emerges. But all this work goes for nothing if the garden ground is not protected from the invasion of rabbits, hares, roe deer, sheep. John Reid said in the seventeenth century 'As there is no country can have more need of planting than this, so non more needful of Inclosing, for we well know how vain it is to plant unless we Inclose'.

One neighbour has planted a hedge of briar rose. The thorns do seem to prevent invasion by sheep, the flowers, of course, are lovely and the hips are the size of tomatoes and can be made into all sorts of preserves. A New Zealander tells me that they make hedges of whin (gorse). That should keep everything out! There is certainly plenty of whin here. In early summer it brightens the whole landscape. At one time growth was encouraged, as whin was used as fodder for the horses when winter supplies were finished. Every place had a 'knocking stone', a hollowed-out stone in which the plants were pounded into a mealy substance. In some parts there were 'whin mills' specially made for the crushing of whins.

Broom, too, makes great splashes of yellow, of a much warmer shade than that of the oilseed rape favoured by the low ground folk. *Ach buidhe*, the yellow field, is a common place-name in the heights.

March 17th

St Patrick's Day! It's good that we should set aside certain days to commemorate the lives of people who left their mark on time. St Patrick, of all the saints, would have felt at home in these hills, I think. So today's a day for the 'wearing of the green' and for hoping that that lovely island of his will find its way again.

Two great men of comparatively recent times were Columba of Iona and Francis of Assisi. Both were men of the world, with inner visions of how good life could be. Both built their citadels in places apart, for both wanted close contact with the natural world, with the cycle of sun and moon, of life and death. Both loved their fellow creatures, animals, plants, all created life. Francis, in particular, called animals and birds his 'brother' or his 'sister'. In Columba's case the love of animals—I'm thinking of his beloved white horse—may have stemmed from very old Celtic beliefs about reincarnation, which have parallels with Hindu beliefs, showing the Indo-European origins of the Celtic peoples.

For the Celts, cattle were the mainstay of life. The bull was practically deified, its great strength and energy making it appear kin to the great god Beli, the father of all life. The cow was regarded as the provider of earthly bounty—fertility, nourishment, clothing. There would appear to be an Indo-European link here, as the cow is the most sacred animal of India.

Cattle were also the mainstay of later Highland people, until the coming of the 'big sheep' towards the end of the eighteenth century. Previously, two or three sheep would have been kept, like pets, perhaps along with a goat or two, to provide wool, meat and milk if the house cow was dry. The cow gave milk, butter, cheese and even, in the hardest times, blood to be mixed with meal for an emergency diet. The country is criss-crossed with drove roads used to take the cattle to far-off markets and many tales are told of the experiences of the drovers.

The last of the cattle have gone now from our hills here, cattle that kept the land in good heart, trampling rough growth, yet eating their fill and manuring copiously. Only the sheep remain, leaving the ground bald with their constant over-grazing. The cows and their followers became almost an extension to the family, having names and recognisable individualities. In very old times, on cold winter nights, when the sound of their munching could be heard through the partition wall, there must have been a close bond between man and beast. Our fields are sad now, rushes and bracken choking the bright grass. The hills where the sheep used to be are now only home to the hare. On the lower slopes, roe deer and pine marten find shelter among the scattered rocks and pine. The fox still roams unhindered and the odd half-wild 'moggy' ventures into chicken runs.

It's good to know these creatures are all about us, though we only catch glimpses of them as they flee. Snow-tracks bring pictures of them to mind: the hare, with his great powerful back legs out-pacing the two at the fore-end, and the fox, with his delicate tread, leaving a small trail of footprints as he sleuths his prey. Up at the loch I've seen the imprint of the fox crossing those of the otter on the snow-covered ice. I've wondered what happened when fox and otter met!

Then there are the tiny footprints of mice and voles, left as they venture out looking for provender in some known cranny. Small waves of wisdom emanate from all forms of life. The deer, the song-bird, the leaf, the flower, they all accept life as it comes and death as it comes. Immortality is a very old human concept, though the Christian form of it is comparatively modern. To the ancient Celts, with beliefs, as it seems, perhaps more akin to those of the Indo-Europeans, it appeared that we all passed through various life-forms during our time on earth, from 'a wave on the sea to a mighty oak', as I've heard it put. We therefore share kinship with every form of life and have much to learn from our fellows. The American Indians had this feeling for life and would ask forgiveness of a tree which had to be felled.

The sad feature of modern times is that urban life cuts people off from the life-forces, even of night and day, of sun and moon. In town, the stars are invisible, snow melts fast, there is shelter from wind and rain. Dependency on man-made devices for survival becomes the norm for daily living.

Nevertheless, people are looking, I think, for contact with other forms of life. Perhaps the only manageable animal companion for the townsman is a dog. Many seem happy today with a dog, often a large, very active dog, sharing their life.

To the Celtic people, the hound was an indispensable ally in the struggle for life, guarding the house, fighting off enemies, helping in the hunt. The sheepdog of today has the same capacity for loyal service, his hunting instincts curbed and transformed into one for herding. Many place-names commemorate the importance of hounds in daily life. Just up the road here there is a hillock, *Tom Choin*, 'the hounds'.

There are also many areas of hill-ground known as *Caiplich*, the place of horses. The horse was another great companion-animal for man. In older times he was endowed with magical qualities and could carry his rider to *Tir nan Og*, the Land of Youth. He could also, in the form of a water-horse, or kelpie, drag him down below the dark waters of a loch. In Ireland the cult of the horse remains, his power of speed being paramount and leading to the breeding of fine racing animals. In the Western Isles, too, there were famous horse-races during the festivities of Michaelmas.

The red deer stag perhaps reigns supreme in the animal world for the Highlander. Huge, powerful and horned, he epitomises the wild natural force that has inspired the generations. He and his hinds lived in the forests in older times, when the forests were of native pine growing in natural spacing, not in thick-set plantations grown commercially. They were said to be the cattle of the fairy folk, supplying them with milk.

The salmon who ate the hazel-nuts of knowledge as they fell into the pool was another symbolic creature for the men of the hills. As they watched the great fish in its tragic struggle to swim upstream to the spawning ground, only to die when its task was accomplished, they saw that this represented the goal of all wisdom, the acceptance of death as the gateway to new life.

The birds of the air must often have caused the people to feel envy as they watched the great wings outspread and the creatures soaring away, seeming to rise above all earthly troubles and cares. Probably in spirit, they journeyed miles with the eagle and the hawk. Certain birds inspired fear. A neighbour of mine still dreads seeing a heron fly near her house. Its slow, sombre wing-beats carry, for her, a premonition of death.

March 28th

Official spring came in a week ago and today it's 'summer time', so we should be feeling like a gambol with the early lambs in the field over the road. But March is the month of hard graft. My diary entries certainly record this. Shifting barrow-loads of dung, still digging and fork-ing out recalcitrant weeds, doing all the donkey-work in preparation for the great days of sowing and planting. This year the work has gone ahead fairly smoothly. Times of snow and gale have been only intermittent and short-lived. One sunny morning a wagtail appeared, running happily along the ridge of the roof. The flowering currant began to blossom in the hedge. Then, the clearest signal of spring—a curlew calling. It's a sad, lonely, quiv-ering call, but it means that these incomparable birds are back. They've left their wintering on the coast and are here to nest and make increase. That's enough to lift the day.

We can cherish our garden birds—clearing snow, breaking ice, to keep them fed and watered. But the birds of hill and moor have to survive in their own way. Sadly, there are fewer of them every year. When spring was a time for ploughing and the work turned up worms and grubs and attracted insects all birds made bonanza. Now the ground is left to insipid pasture with encroachment of rushes, nettles, thistles, every kind of weed. The nettles do help the butterflies and the thistles would delight goldcrests, but these are now so few. And no larks sing here now.

We have one thing to be grateful for, as we look out on our changing landscape. Foresters are abandoning the planting of dense stretches of conifer. 'Bring back the birch' is a welcome slogan today. The birch—from the winter outline of its mauve branches to the May-time greening and the autumn gold, and the year-long shine of the silver bark, it's an incomparable tree. And to think, as a friend said lately, that we used to be told to dispose of the seedlings as weeds! Now it is recognised that, as timber, birch wood is a useful product. Bunches of twig still make good garden besoms, though they're no longer used to punish small boys!

Already, there are several 'amenity' plantings in the neighbourhood, small enclaves of native trees—gean and rowan, with their beautiful blossom and fruit; hazel, with its catkins and nuts. Willow still grows in the damp places, though it's no longer used for making baskets and creels. Larch, not really a native, but a welcome incomer, makes a good protective border and oak flourishes further down the hill. Bird cherry is everywhere, with its lovely blossom and its profusion of fruit, which is edible, but, alas, has too bitter a taste.

APRIL

April 9th

The curlew's call now accompanies all the garden work. There is a feeling of companionship about it. The pair of them must be as hard-worked, over there, in the rushes by the burn, looking for a nest-site, building, warding off rivals, as I am digging, clearing, preparing the way for the year's growth.

Perennial things are moving, but slowly, cautiously, on account of the persistent easterly winds. A breeze from the south-east, for a few days, is welcome, for it normally brings clear skies and some sunshine. But a continuous stream of cold air from the east or north-east is a real deterrent to growth. The early bite of spring grass can be vital at lambing-time. Where are our westerlies, we wonder. They must be blowing somewhere, blowing softly, bringing the small rain. T S Eliot said:

> April is the cruellest month, breeding
> Lilacs out of the dead land . . .

'The cruellest month' . . . I wonder if he really knew how right he was. The vegetable plots are ready now and I'm tempted to sow and plant. But the whisper of experience is there, close to my ear. There's frost to come and lashing rain and all the other enemies of tender plant and burgeoning seed. I know, I know, though it's difficult to believe, when the blackbirds are singing non-stop and the sun is warm on the hands. We must wait a month yet and try for a waxing moon, so it's on with the eternal weeding. Nothing holds back the weeds—chickweed, shepherd's purse, couch grass and sorrel. A farming friend from the low-ground is ridding her fields of corn marigolds, one of my best-loved flowers. We transplanted some last year and I'm fervently hoping they will have seeded.

Meanwhile, the laborious task of clearing is often relieved by the unearthing of strange things. Many times small, discarded, and mostly broken, toys have appeared, the remains of dumps made by former tenants who did not work the garden. These, and bits of broken china and glass, have mostly been disposed of now, over the years. At one time I was gathering pailfuls of burnable cinders, thrown out with the ashes when coal was cheap. They made a grand glowing winter fire!

An interesting find one day was a Lovat Scout badge, perhaps fallen from the lapel of a digger of years ago! My collection of prehistoric scrapers is growing all the time!

April 16th

Easter is past and no tatties are in the ground. But, as Easter is a moveable feast, so, too, is the time for the planting of tatties. They must wait till the ground is ready and, as the weather is often good in autumn, they can be left to mature fairly late.

This is still the time of preparation for all future growth, the time for the most arduous effort of all the year. Diary entries are terse as time and energy are fully expended outdoors. But this is a day which must be recorded, as it was one which really lifted the spirit. The smell of fresh earth, the curlew calling, bees flying free, these things not only lift the spirit but bring a surge of energy to limbs and back. Work goes on overtime, till late sunset.

Working alone, one yet has a sense of companionship, as all life is busy at renewal, bees foraging, birds nesting, trees budding into leaf, early flowers blooming. There's also the knowledge that gardeners everywhere are at the same tasks, the same muscles aching, the same satisfaction in the smile at the end of the day.

I look up as the sound of tractor-work, far off, draws the ear. Over there, across the big loch, in the distance, small white puffs of cloud are appearing over the brown fields. Someone is spreading lime. This is great news, for it means that one field, at least, has not been 'set aside'. Will it be an experiment with oil-seed rape? This is being grown extensively in some places, the oil being made into a source of energy. Lately, a bee-keeper has brought his hives up here to get them away from fields of this crop, as the honey the bees make from it is almost inedible.

The quest for sources of energy is what is destroying the planet. If we must go on for ever moving over land and sea and into far-off space, if we must have machines to take over all the hard labour, then it's imperative that we harness the energy already existing. At almost any time of the year, on the coast or in the islands you will see and hear energy rushing at you at a speed of knots. Those waves crashing to death against the rocks, urged there by a wind roaring that it has nowhere to go, this is energy in the raw that has been expending itself since the beginning of time.

There are hopeful signs that heed is being taken. In Benbecula, in the Hebrides, a giant windmill helps to power a magnificent new school

Drawing back the curtain
I looked out at the morning in disbelief

complex. On Loch Ness I've seen small 'ducks' bobbing about, measuring wave power. Much more could surely be done.

I stretch up, easing those back muscles, then hunker down again, nose near to the weeding. There's quite a comfort about this position, all one's person in close contact with the earth, no head-in-air remoteness. They do say some of our modern ills have come about since we started walking upright!

Inspired by the sight and sound of that far-off tractor-work, I slit open a bag of lime and scatter the contents on the brassica plot. Most of this ground can do with sweetening, even the tattie plot, especially after heavy winter rains have leached it.

In a spell of good weather such as this the work builds up into what seems an indestructible pile. Will one ever demolish it before the next onslaught of gale, late snow or frost comes in to the attack? It's a question, of course, of sorting out priorities. The lime is spread. Ground not tackled in autumn or winter must now be cleared and manured. The weeding of perennials is a job that's with us always. As long as the more ferocious weeds are got out before their roots really bite, the lesser ones must be left for the time being. Dividing of plants, too, and giving portions to friends is a pleasurable activity, but not one of great urgency at the moment. All strength must be concentrated on getting that ground ready for the seed. A spring day generates its own energy. As normal tea-time approaches, I shake the lime from hands and sleeves, go into the house to wash and make a cup of tea. I take it out to drink as I wander round for a listen to evening bird-song.

A slight breeze is rising. I'll spread no more lime today. Then I catch a whiff of something . . . something pleasant, but something that strikes fear, too, at this time, in this weather—the smell of wood-smoke. Again I look to the distance. There, on the moor ground, to the west, smoke is rising and billowing slightly, billowing this way and that, as the breeze takes it. Surely no one would be starting a heath fire at this time of day? It might be a picnic fire. People are tempted out on fine evenings, in early spring, for a picnic supper.

The first drying winds of the year soon make the heather and the dead grass tinder-dry. An innocent disposing of weeds and rubbish, even in an incinerator, can cause havoc if a spark is carried on the wind into a plantation. This happened here some years ago. I have been very wary of wood-smoke ever since. That afternoon I smelt and saw the flames coming steadily nearer the edge of the planting just beyond the field adjoining the house. Probably the bare ground would halt it, I thought. But I wasn't taking any chances. There were no telephones in the houses then. I alerted a neighbour, who went on his bike to the nearest kiosk and within half an hour a squad of firemen were at work. Forestry workers soon joined them and for hours they hosed and battered the flames. Such fires can smoulder for days when they get a hold of the underlying peat. The ground is then pleasantly warm to the feet, but there's always the fear that fire may break out again. The exhausted firemen stood by all night, refreshed in relays by tea and sandwiches. At last, when daylight came, we all got some rest.

'Muir-burn', that is, the burning of the heather, inadequately supervised and outwith certain times in the year, is an offence, punishable by law. This fire, though purely accidental, did a great deal of damage and caused much distress to the people responsible. The memory keeps me on the alert.

I sniff the air. The smoke smell is still discernible, though the actual grey cloud has disappeared. Not quite reassured, I walk up the road to investigate. Nearing the plantation, beyond the heather, by the loch, I hear talking and laughter. Two cars are parked in the lay-by. As I thought, it's a picnic party and the fire is now down to a red glow. There are young people, older people, children, quite a crowd. There must be a safe pair of hands there, I decide.

The walk is rewarding. I find coltsfoot flowering along the roadside ditch and a woodland blackbird is at his evening choir practice. Tomorrow I must have a garden bonfire, a small one, started early and strictly supervised. The ash is so good for all growing things.

April 30th

Today, in the early morning time, with light around the curtains, I heard it. Or was it part of a dream? With opened eyes, I listened hard. It came again, unmistakably: the sound of the cuckoo. It's a reassuring sound. These parts must still be his haven for summer, no matter what the season brings. He's here! Neighbours come on the phone. You heard him? I did. So all's well! Sometimes we see him, too. Like a small hawk, he looks. And we know about his selfish habits. But still he's our welcome guest.

The swallows are the worry. Up till two years ago we had them nesting in a disused shed. All summer they would be flying happily in and out. Later on, a row of fledglings would perch precariously on the electric cable, parents stuffing the small beaks with food and dive-bombing any human venturing past.

Now we look anxiously, hopefully, for them coming, but to no avail. We think of those ghastly Kuwaiti battlefields in the desert. Did the birds mistake pools of oil for pools of water? Did they succumb to sand-storm, wind-storm, hail-storm? How they manage the flight at all has always been a mystery. We miss them sorely.

The starlings don't nest under the eaves now, either. That's something we don't regret, for the young usually found their way into the loft and would often die of starvation. The starling is not my favourite bird. He's noisy and brash and on occasion has had me running into the house to answer a phantom 'phone'! A flock of starlings, one year, caused a black-out, when they perched, tight-packed, on an electric cable up the road.

Another noisy bird is the black-headed gull, but we're so glad to have them back nesting on the island in the loch, when for ten years or so they were absent. Now they rise in a white, screeching cloud, when they're fright-ened. In the evening they fly silently down to the lower fields to feed and later, eerily, in the dusk, they fly back. It's good to have them, for it means there's returning life on the loch. The tufted duck are busy there, too.

MAY

May 1st

I'm up early, not to wash in the dew, but to listen to the cuckoo, to watch for the swallows, to smell the warming earth. Beltane! 'Beil-teine'—the fire of Belus, an ancient god—this was the name of the day in older times. It was the first day of summer and called for a special celebration, after the suffering and uncertainties of winter and spring.

This was a day for positive activity. Great fires were lit on the hill-tops and the cattle driven through them to ensure good health for the year. All the hearth fires were extinguished and re-kindled with a torch from the purifying flame. Sometimes the young men would leap through the flames to show their daring. A great Beltane bannock would be baked and, in some places, a batter of eggs, butter, oatmeal and milk would be cooked on the Beltane fire and some of it spilled on the ground as a libation.

Bannocks would be baked, too, on St Bride's day, February 1st, the first day of spring, at Lammas, August 1st, for the first day of autumn, and at Hallowmas, the first of November, for the first day of winter. These small ceremonials gave a shape to life which was dearly prized.

There will be no Beltane fires today. The hills have to be made to conform to other patterns, when their main function may well be to provide good hunting and shooting. The cattle are no longer taken up to the heights for the summer grazing. Those must have been happy days when the women and young people would stay up in the shieling huts, herding the cattle and making butter and cheese, while the menfolk watched the growing field-crops and re-thatched the roofs of the houses.

The cutting of peats was another happy May-time occasion, when more distant neighbours, some of whom had perhaps not met for months, would join forces to make light of the work, exchanging news and much banter over a dram at the days' end. Many of the peat-banks are now swallowed up in trees, though the old grazings enjoyed the right to 'graze sheep, cut peats and bleach linen'.

Again in May the custom was to visit a healing well. It was firmly believed that these wells had the power to cure and give protection from diseases of many kinds. In the hills not far from here there is the 'red' well, with water which must surely have contained iron. Offerings of coloured threads and scraps of garments were hung on the trees and bushes round about, as propitiation. These can be seen in several places today.

Thinking of these things and with the feel of May in the air I skip non-essential jobs and walk out to a place I remember. It is hidden in a plantation now. Quite blatantly, I trespass, climbing the fence and following a narrow track through the jumble of trees. Disoriented at first by the changed land-pattern, I come to a gap and look round with recognition. Here, once, a stone-age dwelling stood, the outline of the foundation still clearly visible. Here, before the trees were planted, I had come on arrow-heads and a scraping tool on the fresh-turned furrows.

I find my bearings at once and, a few paces further on, I reach what I'm seeking—a small well, half hidden now in overgrowth. Pulling aside the ferns and rushes, I gaze into the water. It's still dark and clear. There's no sign of the small fish reputed to be there, keeping the water pure. But it's pure enough for me. I scoop up a handful and drink it slowly, relishing every drop. I gaze into the water again and put up a small plea, not for healing or protection for myself, but, perhaps, for the earth, for the whole earth which is in more danger than any of us.

I imagine a man of the flints, tired and thirsty from the hunt, coming for a drink of the water, the water that meant life as surely as fire did. As he stooped over the smooth surface and saw his face reflected there, did he stop for a moment to wonder where he came from, where he might be going? I think he did, for he spent so much of his strength hauling those enormous stones and standing them upright, pointing to the sun, moon and stars. That labour did not profit him or his family in any material sense, but it must have given him immense satisfaction.

A curlew rises from the wet slope below the well. My flint man must have heard the marvellous music of its call and watched the perfect pattern of its flight many times, as I listen and watch now. Nothing can really separate us from the past.

So I've had my May morning. I leave no propitiating rags at the well, only a small whisper of thanks, and wander back, deeply refreshed. On the doorstep I find two people waiting. They are young. They look a little weary under the burden of their heavy back-packs. Hesitantly, for the language is not their own, they ask for water for their flasks.

'Of course!' I say 'come and sit on the green while I fill them.' They accept gladly. I tell them of my well and bring them two brimming glasses of water. 'This is from a well, too. My well is away up in the hill there.' 'You are lucky', they say. Then, over copious drinks and a plateful of rock cakes we talk—of the Highlands, the weather, of Austria their homeland and many other things. They will send me a plant for the garden, some edelweiss, they say. I mark on their map the tracks they can take through the hills and wave them off at the gate to the wilderness places they love.

I often remember an old Gaelic rune:

> I saw a stranger yestreen;
> I put food in the eating place,
> Drink in the drinking place
> And, in the sacred name of the Triune
> He blessed myself and my house,
> My cattle and my dear ones,
> And the lark said in her song,
> Often, often, often
> Goes the Christ in the stranger's guise;
> Often, often, often
> Goes the Christ in the stranger's guise.

May 3rd

An invitation to join a family outing to the west is always irresistible. This year the May holiday did not bring the weather one would have wished, but it was pleasant to down tools, pack a picnic and set off. There's always a feeling of growth in the west and of kindness, kindness in the air and in the people. Frost and snow don't linger. The prevailing wind is soft and brings welcome rain. The dry east wind is half spent before it arrives and usually brings the sun. And, of course, there's the Gulf Stream. This time we didn't make for the gardens of world-wide renown at Inverewe, but drew into a quiet, unknown place on the shore of Loch Broom and into the shelter of a huge garden wall. This is a Victorian garden which has passed to various owners over the years. For 45 years, from 1940, it lay unattended. It is now being restored. There was no one about. We found an honesty box for our donations, a leaflet and a map. We followed the path and pushed open an enormous door. It was like entering the realm of the secret garden of childhood days. The lilac was in bloom. There were rhododendrons of colours that took the breath away, trees that had overgrown into the most fantastic shapes, and small, unexpected patches of plants among the rocks. Paths led in all directions. We followed one to the shore, lured by the scent of salt water and seaweed, then back by mysterious ways to the vegetable plots. Here, seaweed was mulching straw-berries. I grew the tatties, one year, on a bed of seaweed. They throve magnificently! Then we came on a real surprise—asparagus! The balm of the west was at work.

There was no tea in the house here, no plant stall, not even a gardener to be seen, but the tortuous little paths, the sudden glimpses of colour, the smell of the sea, the happy entanglement of wild and cultivated growth gave it a feel of mystery and magic which many spruced-up places lack.

Next day, at home, I look on this old garden with new eyes. It's a Victorian garden, too, in its way, with its laurel hedge, its ferns and rhododendrons and statuesque lilies. And it has passed through many hands. For me, it has that touch of mystery which overgrowth and the intrusion of the wilderness brings. I take a wander and a muse and try not to be too busy for a while.

I watch the birds as they fly off with beakfuls of tasty scraps for mates and nestlings. The daffodils will be out any day and the strawberries are beginning to flower.

John Reid, our Scots Gard'ner, tells us, in April, to 'Sow all your annual flowers . . .' and to 'Open the Doors off your bee-hives now they hatch.' But I think, maybe, we've had some climatic change since the 1600s. We're into May now and we'll still leave our sowing yet a little while. I'll take his other advice and 'Fall to your mowing and weeding.'

The grass got its first cutting today!

May 8th

A few days of warm showers and the ground feels really ready for the seed. When you can pick up a handful of earth and let it trickle through your fingers and there's a whiff of damp about, that means it's a day John Reid would have approved of for planting. These days I feel he's often at my back with his couthy comments and advice. But I have to remind him that this is not a laird's garden with labourers to hand.

It's certainly time the tatties were a-bed, so in they go, into a good mixture of manure, with a blessing on their heads. They are Kerr's pinks. I've never found one I like better. Sometimes I wonder who this Kerr was and how he grew his pink potato. With the tatties in, in go the onions. There's the potential making of a good pot of soup. These are two crops which risk little from the garden predators. Only that big cock pheasant has been known to gouge a tattie out of the ground with his large greedy beak.

Cabbage whites and tortoiseshells are on the wing among the dandelions, and the first swallow swoops out of a grey sky high above the roof-top. Will he be back to build? There's the hope. Then, something that really gives a lift to the day—the sound of a peewit. I stop to listen. It comes again. Could it really be a pair prospecting for a nest site, as they used to do? Again, there's a hope.

they will fashion most
beautiful wreaths and garlands

With a great renewal of energy I work on till dusk, sowing the first rows of salad seeds—lettuce, radish, spring onion, carrot. Tomorrow the turnips, then the annual flowers—nasturtium, cornflower, love-in-a-mist. I'll find room for them all somewhere. This year I shall make companion plantings—marigolds among the carrots.

Wandering back to the house I see the grass is shooting up. At this time of the year if you turn your back on one bit of the garden for five minutes or more it gets completely out of hand. You wonder if there will ever be a time when you can walk round appreciating everything without seeing something—an outcrop of weeds, an unpruned bush—that urgently needs doing.

The grass—the word 'lawn' is not really in my garden vocabulary, I prefer to call it the 'green'—I am always reluctant to cut. Let it grow and it's a meadow, a dampish meadow with lots of moss, wild flowers—eyebright, lady's smock, lady's mantle, self-heal, speedwell, stitchwort, hawkbit, bird's foot trefoil, buttercups and daisies. And mushrooms in season, even chanterelles. Over the years it has given so much to the life of the house—picnics, nights out in a 'bivvy' to catch the early sights and sounds, sunbathing and football games. This year I shall cut a good patch in the middle for the ball games and leave wide swathes round the edges for the flowers.

May 15th

Today, drawing back the curtains, I looked out at the morning in disbelief. I thought it was a dream. I rubbed my eyes and looked again. It was reality. There was a white garden out there, a spring garden lying under snow, quietly accepting its fate. And the day before I had enjoyed the first real leisurely outdoor tea-break of the year. I clear a path to the gate. By mid-morning the wind is rising and more snow falling heavily. The blackbird is singing his heart out in the blizzard. I bless him for his brave reassurance. But the snow is still falling, sleety at times, then in heavy flakes again. With night there will be frost. Stories are circulating of folk snowed up, of cars stuck on the hill. There is great discussion about climatic change, global warming, a new ice age. Then we remember: only a few years ago there was a snowfall in early June! So it's just our eccentric weather at its tricks again.

The blossom on the bird cherry is miserably bedraggled, the daffodils that cheer the high places are flattened, only the low-growing plants and herbs stay happy under their strange covering. Then the wind veers to the east. It brings no clear skies, but cloud and a chill mist, so growth in everything is halted. And the east wind goes on blowing.

May 19th

If April is the cruellest month, May, so far this year, is not much kinder. Still, the tatties and the first sowings of vegetables are in the ground, though they'll be wise enough to bide their time before emerging. Curlew and pee-wit are calling down the wind, their flight patterns hidden in the mist. It's a day for feeling restless, perhaps for a foray down the road, instead of up, to see what signs of growth are on the way.

The birches are greening and in the hollow by the burn there's the gleam of celandine. Chaffinches are singing non-stop and a thrush is shouting from the top of the highest pine. Lambs are leaving their mothers's sides to gang up with their siblings and try out their skills at racing and butting. There's life enough to defy whatever the weather can devise.

I turn off the road and wander through what was once a busy settlement. The houses are fewer now, for they are bigger, the people in them not depending on their surroundings for a living. But some of the little abandoned gardens can still be seen. The little old houses would have had a few flowers growing near the door, but the word 'garden' would have meant a small plot, walled with stone for protection from the wind and predators, on the edge of the ground cultivated for the main crops of the croft—oats, hay, turnips, potatoes. In the garden would be grown ingredients for the soup-pot—carrots and kale and some soft fruit for puddings and preserves.

Some years ago, when there was no one living in these parts, I came on one such garden, a long, narrow stretch beside the burn. Rhubarb plants had grown to the size of small trees, there were blackcurrant bushes drastically overgrown, but alive, and gooseberries still bearing yellow fruit. I took cuttings of these and now have half a dozen good bushes fruiting happily. Gooseberries and blackcurrants were always part of the summer diet and made valued winter preserves. Raspberries were gathered wild, for puddings and also for jam. Wild mint and wild garlic were everywhere. This little garden must have had a really devoted gardener, for in one corner was a lilac and in another a gean.

I wandered on down the track to inspect a certain hollow tree, a very ancient, gnarled hawthorn, for here, I was told, a colony of honey bees, a lost swarm, had been nesting for years. Had they survived this long period of cold and wet, I wondered. There was no sight or sound of them. I drew closer and looked into the hollow. There was wax, untidy wax, and some bee corpses, but, alas, no sign of living bees. Perhaps, I hoped, they had moved elsewhere last summer. A nearby landowner once sold some ground to a neighbour on condition that he agreed never to cut down a certain tree in which bees had been nesting for two hundred years. Would that conditions like that were laid down more often! I thought of my pampered bees, fed icing-sugar and covered with strips of old blanket. Perhaps these things act as sops to my conscience for robbing them every year of their surplus stores!

A young hare springs from almost under my feet. He wouldn't have found much joy in this old garden today, but his forebears would have had many a tasty treat. Before the days of wire fencing total protection of crops was well-nigh impossible. A leap or a scramble could take predators of all kinds over a wall, unless it were six feet high. Thinking of this, my thoughts went out and back, through the years, to the crofter's wife who cherished this plot.

Little walled plots like it are everywhere, turfed over now, beside ruined croft houses. One such, up the road and past the loch, where a single tree now stands sentinel, took the laird's prize for the best-kept garden on the estate. Now that new people are in the old houses, little sheltered plots are most often swept away, in favour of landscaped areas, planted with flowering trees and shrubs. These are very pleasant places, too, reflecting new ways of living and working.

I wander back to my own portion of earth, I mean the bit I have on loan from the planet, refreshed by this foray into the past. I'm glad of the links with former times. I can see the look of distress that clouded and wrinkled that woman's face, when she went out to gather kale for the soup and found it lying in shreds on the wet ground. I've found devastation like that. But to give up growing for the kitchen would be unthinkable. No supermarket greenstuff can ever compare with what you gather on a bright morning from your own plot. Tatties dug and boiled within the hour make a feast for any epicure.

In the evening, warmed by thoughts of the past, I switch thoughts to the future. Tomorrow, weather willing, will be the time to confront the problems of this reluctant spring.

May 23rd

The wind is still in the east and there have been spells of drizzle, but the ground is drying out a little. Lettuce, radish and onions are through the ground and the peas look healthy, so there must have been a dearth of the wee mice that sometimes decimate the crop. One year I tried everything— black pepper, sprigs of furze, anything to deter the hungry little rascals, as I re-sowed and re-sowed the peas. The rest of the vegetable seeds, turnip, beetroot, American land cress, will have to take their chance of being washed out of the ground by a sudden onslaught of rain from the north-east. Chinese cabbage is best sown late, to prevent it shooting. The wildflower seeds should surely be hardy. They went in in a waxing moon.

One great pleasure to be relied on every year, come any kind of weather, is the appearance of the garden's own secret flowering. During our first year here we let the garden have its own say. We knew there would be flowering currant and raspberries. We were not disappointed. And yellow raspberries? They were all appreciated, with dollops of cream. But the flowers—they were to surprise us. Aquilegia, granny's bonnets, have seeded everywhere and in the most beautiful range of colours—mauve, deep purple, pink, blue. Neighbours come to look at them with envy! Then there are the Welsh poppies, bright splashes of yellow after the daffodils have gone; periwinkle, that even risks the winter cold; London pride (a favourite of Gertrude Jekyll) and woodruff, making a delicate ground-cover in the half-shade under the trees. Forget-me-nots are cherished, and Honesty, with its promise of autumn silver. Foxglove flowers everywhere, in quiet corners and in the herbaceous border. Sweet cecily, of course, rampages, valiantly resisting any attempt at cut-backs.

Now, over the last few years, there have been some really astonishing surprises. The sudden appearance of poppies, enormous poppies, in great profusion, and of all shades of mauve and pink, brought neighbours to admire and to beg for seed. How they came is a mystery. We accept their presence with great joy. Every year they appear, even among the brassicas or the onions. This year they are in the salad bed. I weed carefully to keep as many as possible. Another mysterious arrival is a most beautiful clump of eryngium, blue-stemmed and blue-headed, the envy of dried-flower arrangers. I have no recollection of having planted them.

Beyond the garden wall, in the grass-grown yard, is a very special flower—the purple orchid. The old walls themselves carry their own small flowerings. In the secret crevices stonecrop grows happily along with toadflax and bright mosses.

Even with vicious east winds and cold mist May is still the season of forward-looking days. Everything will right itself in the end, we feel. The weeds are certainly never inhibited by the worst the weather can bring. Shepherd's purse and sorrel are growing apace, many small seedlings showing up among the rows of vegetables. Every year I vow to hoe before any new weed grows big enough to be absorbing the nutrients meant for food crops. I never quite achieve this, but I try! I remember Robert Louis Stevenson's lines 'To a Gardener':

> Friend, in my mountain-side demesne
> My plain-beholding, rosy, green

And linnet-haunted garden-ground
Let still the esculents abound.

I had to consult a dictionary for 'esculents'. It means food plants. I hope
my esculents are happy!

JUNE

June 1st

A dry day, but a cold one. The siskins are still coming to the nuts at the window. I should really wean them off, in case they give up looking for their natural food. They are so attractive to watch. Perhaps I'm being selfish.

A morning walk up the garden shows me the tatties are through the ground. A reason to celebrate! The failure of the potato crop often meant near starvation in the old Highlands. Their progress is still closely watched, with a touch of anxiety, even today. People still living remember when a pot of tatties, turned out straight on to the scrubbed kitchen table and eaten with the fingers with a knob of butter when the cow was in milk, was a sumptuous midday meal. I look forward to my first dish of tatties, dry and crumbly, the 'apples of the earth'.

The grass is growing fast now. Soon I must take the mower to the green again, though I'm always reluctant to cut back those first bright shoots and the incipient stalks of wild flowers. I wander up to the strawberry patch. An orange-tip is there before me, flitting from flower to flower. That seems like another good omen.

This is a time of waxing moon, a propitious time for planting. Older Highland people still watch the moon closely, in all its phases, for weather predictions, days appropriate for certain activities and so on. The waning moon is good for ploughing and peat-cutting, for the 'sap' is going, leaving everything dry. An old lady will still walk clockwise three times round the house at the first appearance of the new moon. People don't like to see the half moon 'lying on her back'. This is a bad omen. Looking up at 'Paddy's lantern' on a winter's night one wonders just how clever they could be?

The waxing moon being a good time for setting out on a journey, I go down to give a gardening hand to a friend who is crippled by arthritis. Between us we clear the small plots along the front of the house, where nettles and creeping buttercup are threatening his roses. These roses, pale pink and deep red, are a delight later on and the envy of his neighbours. At one time climbers covered the whole wall. I also envy him his blue irises and the mass of crocuses and primulas which he grows for his beloved bees. The weeds eradicated, we put pansies from our local nursery in every available space. There will be colour against the grey stone wall till well into the autumn.

Down the south-east-facing slope below the house there is a vegetable garden which would have provided everything for the soup pot when the family was growing—carrot, cabbage, swede, kale—and blackcurrants and raspberries for jam. Still the rhubarb is healthy and the old trees sport apples and damsons when they feel like it. Now this small plot looks a little like the 'Gudeman's Croft', a small piece of land dedicated to the 'Gudeman', a kind of earth spirit, which was sacrosanct and not to be touched by plough or spade. There are one or two such spots up my way! I call it Permaculture!

A quick cup of tea and I'm back home to catch an hour or two of waxing moon for a planting. I usually indulge in the purchase of a few brassica plants from our nursery in case the seedlings already in the ground should fail. In go some cabbage and purple-sprouting broccoli. The cabbage is often wrongly maligned, I think. Raw, in a winter salad, or lightly cooked and eaten with a sprinkling of pepper and a dash of butter, it is supremely good. The broccoli, of course, lasts the winter through and is as good a stand-by as kale. Now it's good to see a row of 'greens' looking so sturdy at this time of year, even though there was a slight cheating involved.

After supper, with the urge to plant still strong, I go out, in the quiet evening, to sow another row of calendula between the lines of carrot seedlings. Companionship certainly won't do any harm, though the flowering may be late.

A leisurely stroll back through the herb plots is always a pleasure, especially in the evening, when there's the scent of lavender and balm. Stooping to pick a leaf of sage I look round with care. Weeds are appearing. Couch grass is shooting up even in the middle of that clump of lemon-scented thyme. I dug it up last year, cleared it of weeds, as I thought, divided and replanted it. A truce is out of the question with weeds. It has to be war. Buttercups are creeping, clover too, and even that dreaded horse-tail here and there.

Normally there's not much worry with the herbs. They spread and grow close so that there's little room for intruders. But it's when most of your time is spent sowing or planting in other parts that they sneak in. Sometimes I think of the Zen garden I saw once, in Glasgow, at the St Mungo centre. Stones of varying shapes and sizes are interspersed with finely raked white gravel. Not a weed is to be seen, not a flower either. There is nothing to distract eye or ear. It is purely a place for contemplation, meditation. As such it has much to offer in times of noise and stress. But . . . a garden?

Did God establish that first one 'east in Eden' ? It had an apple tree. To enter the world of Tir nan Og, the Land of Youth, the heaven of the Celts, one carried a branch of the apple tree, laden with blossom or fruit. I know

a white foxglove stands,
tall and straight

the magic of my own old apple tree, when the blossom shines against the summer sky.

June 8th

A June day at last! This year they have to be counted in ones, or, at the most, twos. With the warmth, of course, out come the midges. Scratching the bites being impossible, with dirt-filled fingernails, much time is wasted going indoors to wash and apply layers of lotion. Even this is not totally effective. Gardening friends have invested in masks which, though expensive, do seem to keep the creatures at bay, I have tried my bee-veil, but the mesh is not fine enough for the midge.

Whatever the weather, nothing, not even the threat of snow on the high hills, can deter the weeds. Shepherd's purse is the main offender this year. The tantalising little white flowers stick up in the rows of carrot and beetroot and have to be removed singly, by hand. Whatever happened to that beautiful bare brown ground of sowing time, you wonder. Gardening magazines and the television screen show pictures of lovely weedless earth. Is there a magic we have missed?

This is the time of year when the whole garden seems to take over and resists all attempts to tame it. As one row of seedlings is cleared of shepherd's purse another begins to disappear in clumps of chickweed. Clover creeps into the strawberry bed and sorrel clutters damp patches everywhere. Nettles and dockens do confine themselves to the edges, but something akin to a machete is needed to clear a path up to the orchard.

Everything is late in flowering this year, but the blue geranium never fails to cheer and this day the first of the oriental poppies burst into flame.

June 9th

Thursday, St Columba's day, said to be the best day for making a start at anything—that's today! A cowherd in South Uist gave Alexander Carmichael, the great collector of Celtic lore, a poem about this. It runs:

> Thursday of Columba benign,
> Day to send sheep on prosperity,
> Day to send cow on calf,
> Day to put the web in the warp.
>
> Day to put coracle on the brine,
> Day to place the staff to the flag,

> Day to bear, day to die,
> Day to hunt the heights.
>
> Day to put horses in harness,
> Day to send herds to pasture,
> Day to make prayer efficacious,
> Day of my beloved, the Thursday,
> Day of my beloved, the Thursday.

I can't let the day go by without a salute to St Columba. He passed this way some 1,400 years ago and has left his mark in the remains of his settlement down by the big loch. The sanctified ground extended well beyond the initial boundaries. At one time the whole area was considered a sanctuary, though it is not marked out, as it was in Applecross. A sanctuary meant safety in a place beyond the reach of the law or the sword. It is said that in this place some MacDonalds sought refuge after the massacre in Glencoe. It is certain that the name MacDonald is still the oldest here and it was that borne by the bard, Thomas, and by many skilled masons of his family, who worked the granite and whinstone of the area.

Columba's island, Iona, is a magic place even today. He came from Ireland and soon settled to become an islander, though he and his followers made many forays overseas. I understand his love of the place, for an island gives one a sense of wholeness, of circumscription. One is held by the surrounding sea, but not limited by it. It bathes one round in reassurance, yet it beckons, too. It carries pictures, visions, of boundless, unnamed possibilities, not outwith one's grasp. I think that's how St Columba and his followers must have felt.

It is sometimes difficult to remain whole on the mainland. I try to visit an island every summer. I come home wearing what my friends call my 'island smile'. I think it means I've had a taste of honeydew and maybe a sip of that 'milk of paradise'. Hardy knew about this. He put it this way:

> When I came back from Lyonnesse
> With magic in my eyes . . .

I certainly have in my mind's eye the sight of those flowers on the machair and I still hear the sounds of the birds and the seals.

Now back to today, St Columba's day, and for me it's going to be a 'day to find plants for healing', for healing and for health. Within walking distance, I'm sure, there are wild plants here for treating all the common ailments and most of the more serious ones, and also for promoting health in general.

I take the road up to the hill loch, always a favourite summer walk. Here, in late spring, the little 'wind flowers' always delight us with their surprise appearance. As they fade, the primroses arrive. Some forty or fifty years ago, when the scholars went on foot to school, often barefoot in the summer to 'get the feel of the ground', they would while away the walking time sucking the primrose stems. 'As good as sweeties', they would say. They are still blooming, in this early summer time, tucked away in damp, cool spots between the road and the trees. They can certainly cure a child's longing for sweet things.

Coming to the shelter of the trees, we find the delicate wood sorrel still in bloom. This sensitive small plant loves shade. The clear green leaves, very like those of the shamrock, will close up if touched, as will the flowers, at night. An infusion of the plant can be used as a gargle and it's said that, externally, it helps to cure scabies.

As we reach the loch the scent of bog myrtle is rising from the damp ground. It grows in such profusion that I can happily gather a bunch. In a jar on the kitchen windowsill it acts as a deterrent to flies and wasps. Next I look for that supreme provider of cures—the meadowsweet. It's there, in its accustomed place, stems and leaves appearing. It will flower later in the summer. It deserves its name 'queen of the meadows', for its properties are many. Its fragrance made it a 'strewing herb' in older times. About a hundred years ago, it was used in the formulation of a drug to control fevers which was called aspirin, after the plant's botanical name 'spirea'. It has anti-inflammatory properties, so is helpful to sufferers of rheumatism. Its tannin content can cure cases of diarrhoea. It has an antiseptic action and also contains vitamin C. It really is a miniature 'pharmacopeia'.

The usual formula for most herbal remedies is one large handful of the dried plant to two cups of water, simmered for a few minutes, then allowed to steep, preferably overnight. Many herbs can be eaten fresh and raw, which is probably what nature intended, or they can be chopped finely and steeped in cold milk, a tablespoonful to a cup. Often, as I walk around the garden, going from job to job, I pick a handful of feverfew, leaf and flower, to chew on, though I'm lucky enough not to suffer from bad headaches. Thinking about it now, perhaps this habit is the reason why!

Coming home by the path that snakes through the moor ground, I find another great cure-provider—the tormentil. It is good for assuaging toothache, the great 'torment'. Also, the root is astringent and was used at one time in tanning.

I reach the garden and think again of Columba and his followers as I bend to the weeding. They had weeds to contend with, I'm sure, for everything would flourish in that small island. It is windswept but seldom frost-bitten, and the machair ground is rich in calcium. In my patch the never-ending battle is with couch grass, shepherd's purse and chickweed, yet even these can be beneficial. Cats and dogs eat grass to cleanse their systems. In humans the roots of couch grass, those long, white, fleshy roots we love to hate, can be used to treat gall-stones, kidney and bladder infections. A tablespoonful of small pieces to one and a half cups of water is simmered briefly, then allowed to steep and taken with honey, one cup in the morning, one at night. Shepherd's purse can be used as a first-aid treatment to check bleeding. A cloth soaked in a brew (a dessertspoonful to a cup of water) of the whole plant can be applied to a wound. Chickweed cures many ailments, internal and external. Eat a handful raw twice a day to make a healing agent for inflammation of the whole of the digestive system. Apply the herb fresh, after washing, to sores on the skin and it will draw out impurities.

Even a small understanding of the properties of all these plants helps us to look more kindly even on those which invade our 'cultivated' crops.

There are so many more—the rose, the raspberry, ladies' mantle, eyebright, the list is almost endless. We have our ancestors to thank for the patient experimenting they must have undertaken before discovering the cures they needed. It's good that we are now rediscovering them and appreciating the wisdom of former ways.

June 15th

Another summer day to celebrate! A cool wind from the east brings a cloudless sky and bright sun. It's not quite warm enough for breakfast on the green, but the afternoon tea-break will surely be taken there.

The bees are out early. Every day I walk up through the willowherb, now grown tall and sturdy, with flower-spikes beginning to colour, to inspect the hive. Every day I hope to find the happy, busy flying of bees in and out. There are bees flying, but not in the numbers expected at this time. They won't be swarming, that's one thing sure. A swarm in June is 'worth a silver spoon', the old saying goes. Some years ago I had several hives and could happily give swarms to neighbours. Today the important thing is to keep my few precious bees alive. I remember the time when they died, unbelievably, in early summer. To work about the garden with no humming of bees brought such a sense of unreality and loss that I scoured the countryside looking for someone's surplus hive, begging for a swarm. Eventually I found a beekeeper with a nucleus for sale. I brought it home in triumph in the back of a friend's car and got a hearty stinging as I fitted the newcomers into my old hive. They've adapted and built themselves into a reasonable colony now and are a most precious asset. I'll slip another chunk of last year's honey into the hive to make sure they don't starve. It seems absurd to be feeding bees in the summer, but the weather has been so unpredictable—snow in May and gales and heavy bursts of rain—that the good has been largely washed out of the flowers. The late flowering plants may have escaped and the heather is still to come. So we still hope there may be a little surplus honey for our winter toast.

Feeling that this may be our one and only summer's day I decide to celebrate with the bees. No weeding today! Instead, I go in search of birch twigs for the peas to climb. Already the little delicate tendrils are groping for support. There's no lack of branches, for so many were brought down by the winter gales. And they're easily trimmed. I sharpen the ends slightly and slip them gently into the ground between the row of mange-tout and the row of green peas. It's good to be doing a positive job.

The next salute to summer is to take a slow walk round the whole garden, into each small secret, hidden corner, looking into a flower here, into the incredible structure of an aquilegia, for instance, stooping for the scent of the pinks by the gate, standing to watch the bees going from bloom to bloom in the blue geranium.

This is a day, if ever there was one, for the garden to be enjoyed. I stretch out on the green, hands clasped behind my head, gaze up and send a small canticle of thanks into the blue.

June 21st

The longest day—midsummer! I'm promised a touch of happy madness in the day today, for it's the day of the Garden Party. There will be no cucumber sandwiches, grey toppers or flowered gowns. In the afternoon some young people will arrive, wearing jeans, strong boots and coloured tops. They will disperse, across the moor, into the wood, up the road and soon reappear carrying birch twigs, flowers and grasses. On the patch of rough meadow between the garden and the yard they will set up a pole, fixed firmly into the ground. Then, with birch twigs interlaced with flowers they will fashion most beautiful wreaths and garlands and hang them from a cross-bar near the top of the pole. The whole structure will be festooned in all its length. There will be much laughter and talking in various tongues. This is to be a Scandinavian celebration of summer.

I go up to take the workers a cooling drink. The day is not brilliant but at least it's dry and calm. 'Just like Sweden!' they say. I stand back to admire their handiwork. It really is amazing. I look up and understand. This is surely the christianised version of the maypole. I remember how wise the

early christianisers were to take over pre-christian customs—the venera-
tion of wells, for instance—and this, the acknowledgement of the power
of the sun to bring out life in everything on earth—humans, animals, plants.
In northern lands in particular the warmth and light of the sun are valued
above all else. In Sweden, at the approach of the winter solstice in December, a young girl, wearing a head-dress of lighted candles, will walk through
all the rooms of the house, bringing light into every corner. This festival is
dedicated to St Lucy, Lucia, the saint of light.

Now, six months from the winter solstice, the light is at its zenith. In
the Scottish Highlands the sun was venerated well into Christian times. It is
said that, even barely a hundred years ago, old men in the Islands would
uncover their heads when they first saw the sun in the morning. In the
evening, at sunset, they would again remove their head-covering and bow
their heads to the ground, and say a prayer —

> I am in hope, in its proper time,
> That the great and gracious God
> Will not put out for me the light of grace
> Even as thou dost leave me this night.

This was recorded by Alexander Carmichael in the middle of the last
century. The sun is not showing its brilliance this day, but we have the
assurance that there, beyond the cloud cover, is warmth enough to keep
things growing.

In early evening, the work-day over, more people arrive, parents and
children. They set up a charcoal burner and soon a barbecue is under way.
When appetites are satisfied and all greetings and news exchanged, the real
celebration begins. To the music of fiddle and pipe we dance round the
garlanded pole, holding hands and singing. The words may be Swedish or
Danish, Norwegian or Scots. We all follow the gist and the tune. Some of
the children do an action song. The words may be strange to most of us,
but the meaning is plain. Song after song and dance after dance we do, till
the sky miraculously clears and the sun gives us a farewell gleam, almost as
though on cue. The western sky will scarcely have faded when the east will
begin to shine. There's not much rest for the sun, the eye of the great God,
at this time. We send him a small salute of thanks as we say our good-nights
and goodbyes till next year.

I leave the pole, with its garlands, till the flowers fade. When, eventually,
the time comes to discard them and put the pole away, the feel of that
evening comes back, clear and fresh. I see a farmstead in Norway, small
mixed woodlands surrounding the fields, orchards with blossom and fruit

flourishing in the shelter. Perhaps, one day, we shall have native trees in the Highlands again—birch, hazel, rowan, alder, gean. We could do with another Norse invasion, a friendly one this time, from those friendly Norse cousins of ours—an invasion of ideas!

June 23rd

A day of humdrum jobs—weeding, staking drooping plants, watering seedlings—and any gardener would surely begin to wonder—is this drudgery? Where's the magic now? It will surely be back tomorrow, after a good night's sleep. But . . . when supper's done I go outside. Shall I gather the rhubarb for jam? Even the thought of that succulence on a winter scone seems to lack relish. The midges are not biting. The sky is fading to a duck-egg green. Not even the palest star is to be seen. Of course, we're just past midsummer and . . . this is the eve of St John. Surely a time for celebration. The good saint gave his name to so many healing plants. And he was a wandering man, leaving his footprints in the hot, red desert sand.

I look around. Over the garden wall, among the heather and the seedling birch, a white foxglove stands, tall and straight. A garden escape. It's like a signal. I scale the wall and make across the moor ground to the remains of what was known as the witch's house. Here, in a single room with a leaking roof of thatch, lived an old lady, perhaps eccentric in her ways, but with much goodness in her heart and patience with the young. I salute her memory and walk on.

Crossing the burn, I make back to the road. In the plantations the trees grow too close for access. I remember sometimes, somewhat sadly, the great broadleaved forests in France, where birds sing and flowers grow in the glades. These serried ranks of conifers are gloomy. Even the fire-breaks grow only the rankest grass. But they are a refuge for some forms of wildlife. There is shelter from wind and rain and some warmth in the dry pine-needles. Once, in full daylight, I caught a glimpse of a pine marten crossing the road before disappearing among the dark pine-trunks.

I wander on, all sense of time forgotten, tiredness gone. The night air is scented with bog myrtle. Suddenly, there's the sound so seldom heard these days—the vibrating sound of snipe rising. I catch sight of one in zig-zag flight, silhouetted against the fading sky. It brings back memories of the days when all this ground was alive with birds—with nesting curlew and plover, with redshank, mallard and oyster-catcher and all the small summer birds. Now the pattern of cultivation has changed so drastically we are deprived of these lives.

I reach the woodland by the loch. Here the trees are less dense. I move cautiously. Footfalls are noiseless on the thick carpet of pine-needles. This

A sleek, dark body scrambles ashore

is the time for wildlife to be on the move, when their world is their own
and they can go about their business as they will. Foxes are hereabouts, I
know. There is the snapping of a twig. Looking up into the thickness of
the wood I glimpse a slender brown form disappearing through the trees.
The grace of movement is unmistakable. A roe hind. She may have a
young one near. Have I deprived her of a drink? I move on slowly. She'll
be back.

Reaching a dry spot near the water's edge, I sit down in a natural hide
of fallen branches. The water is calm, reflecting the last tinges of yesterday's sunlight, as today's moves imperceptibly round by the north, hardly
fading in its slow course. I gaze across the water. Mallard, tufted duck,
coot, little grebe will be safely nesting in the rushes on the far shore.
There is a certain eeriness about the water, lying there so still in the half
light. Could this be the calm before a storm? I remember how certain
older folk were reluctant to pass by the loch after nightfall. Was there a
kelpie lurking there in the peaty depths? On this particular night the su-
pernatural seems incredibly real.

I lean back, eyes half closed. A ripple on the surface of the water is
spreading into a wider and wider ring. Have I missed the surge of a kelpie?
There is no creature to be seen. It would have been a fish lured to jump by
a passing cloud of night flies. Something flickers against my face. Not a
bird, surely? It comes again. Of course, a bat, several bats. Feeling happily
absorbed into the night life of the loch shore, I draw a deep breath and
close my eyes.

When I open them again the whole sky is suffused with pale pink light.
The water is still dark and smooth but, close at hand, a ripple is emerging.
Moments later a small dark head appears. A miniature kelpie? Of course
not. A sleek, dark body scrambles ashore and makes for the sandy patch
where a burn enters the loch. Totally unaware of me, the otter searches
about for his breakfast, uttering soft whickering sounds, as though calling
to his family. None appears and he moves swiftly off and disappears into
the deep water. Wild swans I had seen many times on the loch and once,
unbelievably, a storm-strayed cormorant. This is my first glimpse of an
otter on shore, going about his business.

A small flotilla of mallards comes nosing out of the rushes on the far
side. A heron flies in with great slow wing-beats, and stands, an elegant
grey statue, eyeing the shallows. A fox will be standing somewhere, bright-
eyed, too, though I can't see him. This is the time to be about, I think, as,
reluctantly, I slip out of my hide. Walking slowly back by the road I hear
a faint squeaking from the tumble of stones by the dyke. As I stop to
watch, a mother stoat emerges, carrying a minute young one in her mouth.

She will be shifting her family to safer quarters, obeying her own sure instincts. I wish her luck and pass on.

As I reach the house the sun is climbing steadily into a sky that changes almost imperceptibly from pink to pale green, to deeper and deeper blue. I look at the clock. In human time it is still only a quarter past five. Completely refreshed by my outdoor sleep, but exceedingly hungry, I make tea and a plateful of egg on toast and go out to my deserted garden. The flowers are incredibly lovely in the early light. There are long, low shadows across the green. Things should always be seen in a new perspective from time to time. Swallows are chattering overhead, in busy flight. The magic is back!

The weeds are still there, of course, among the growing esculents, as Stevenson calls the food plants. I'm useless with a hoe, knocking out almost as many seedlings as weeds. So it's down on my knees with a hand-fork and a will for a long day's work! This is St John's Day now. Any aches or pains will surely vanish when I remember the flowers of his plant, steeped in olive oil, made a cure much prized by the Crusaders.

Bed, that evening, seems a very stuffy place to be. I shift uneasily, tossing off cumbersome covers. I remember the time in the shelter beside the loch, the timeless time, when night and day merged in one smooth continuum. Is that what is meant by eternity? To have no clocks or watches, no signals of any kind breaking time up into neat segments, this is an enormous relief. The old sun knows what he's doing as he roams around the north sky, waiting to reappear in the east. The animals, flowers, trees, all of life responds to him. It's good to get out of our human capsule and to take a look at what our other earthly neighbours are up to.

As I drift into sleep I resolve to have the children up, to share in a night-time outing—to let them hear the owls' cry and to watch the smooth, dark gliding of wings out of the shadows. At first light fox, pine marten or roe deer may well cross our path. At the loch fish will jump and, with luck, an otter may emerge.

The children will instinctively learn to move in silence, to look, to listen, to be on constant alert, as the animals are. Awareness will grow. On the way back they'll stop to watch the fuzzy caterpillar make his sure way to safety on the grass verge, to see how the daisy—the 'day's eye'—slowly opens its petals to the light.

Reaching home, they'll eat ravenously and by afternoon a sleep on the green will seem like bliss. Waking, with all their energy restored, I think they'll agree that summer nights are too good to waste in bed.

JULY

July 1st

A glorious morning leads in the month, when, surely, the esculents must abound. Radishes, lettuce thinnings, spring onions, land cress, chives and parsley make a memorable first salad of the summer. Soon there will be strawberries for dessert. The plants are full of leaf this year so that the fruit is quite well hidden from the family of blackbirds which have neighboured me all year. If they're deprived of fruit I compensate by throwing out crumbs for them, even though it's (supposedly) summer.

Singling lettuces is a pernickety job, but I fill any available space with the tiny plants in the hope that they'll provide late salads. Strangely enough, I usually find them slow to develop and often have to use several at a time. Kale is a crop that never fails. I'm always glad to be able to give thinnings to a neighbour. He also takes turnip thinnings from me and, to everyone's amazement, they grow and thrive. Kale is delicious, lightly steamed and served with butter. Young turnip, thinly sliced, is good to eat raw and, of course, is the making of a stew or summer soup.

We're lucky, here, to be well out of the way of garden thieves, indeed, to have nothing with commercial appeal, not a gnome in sight! I did, once, from the bedroom window, hear the ecstatic comments of a lady helping herself to an armful of honeysuckle from plants trailing over the wall. As she sped off in her shiny car I smiled and wished her happy smelling. Perhaps she took cuttings that grew. I hope so.

Now that the tatties are 'filling the drills', earthed up and looking promising, the peas are staked and the greens singled, it feels almost as though the esculents are winning. But, of course, we know that there's no off season for chickweed and shepherd's purse is endlessly productive.

The carrots are slow this year, though the marigolds and spring onions I sowed as guard crops are doing well. The beetroot is suffering from the proximity of those glamorous poppies which I'm always tempted to keep growing. Friends come specially to admire them and to ask for seed, attaching labels to the heads they most admire.

One wild flowering I'm missing this year is the white, silky heads of the bog cotton in the damp ground by the loch. Some years it's like a huge drift of snow. A bunch kept in a waterless vase will last two winters through. In older times the heads were used as stuffing for pillows.

July 8th

An evening so cold that the windows were 'steamed', as though with frost! The wind is in the east now, which means a chance of clearer skies and even some sun. The bees are encouraged, though warily. They have a feel for the weather more accurate than that recorded by all the technology down south, and a solid instinct for survival. This means that they're having to consume most of what they make in order to stay alive. There may not be much surplus this year, I'm afraid.

The 'green' is sporting its crop of wild flowers—bird's eye, bedstraw, bird's foot trefoil, hawkweed, lady's mantle. I'm tempted to let them all grow on and have a meadow. But space is needed for ball games when the children come, so the mower must be applied whenever a dry spell allows. I like what Hudson said: 'I am not a lover of lawns, rather would I see daisies in their thousands, ground ivy, hawkweed and even the hated plantain with tall stems, and dandelions with splendid flowers and fairy down, than the too well-tended lawn'.

Wild flowers, I suppose through years of adaptation, seem to do well whatever the weather brings. This summer, in particular, the yellow bedstraw is thriving along the roadside as never before. It's a particularly delicate shade of yellow and so feathery a structure. I'd love to have seen Laurie Lee's mother's garden which he describes so well in *Cider with Rosie*:

> Our terraced strip of garden was Mother's monument, and she worked it headstrong, without plan. She would never clear or control this ground, merely cherish whatever was there; and she was as impartial in her encouragement to all that grew as a spell of sweet, sunny weather. She would force nothing, graft nothing, nor set things in rows; she welcomed self-seeders, let each have its head, and was the enemy of very few weeds.

July 20th

An early phone call carries an invitation to an evening visit to a friend's garden. It's one I have seen evolving over the years, from the slope of an overgrown field, edged with thistles and bracken, to a place of colour and enchantment. It has superb surrounding features—massive slabs of rock, a waterfall in the adjoining gully, overhung with huge oaks, a birch glade and a view down the loch to near and distant hills.

Quite clearly this was a place for a garden on the heroic scale and luckily it found the gardener it needed. The approach to the house carries a hint of mystery. Leaving the road, you cross a cattle-grid, with its hedgehog escape, and enter what has become almost a tunnel, as the bordering shrubs and trees encroach. This evening, as I emerge from the tunnel, I turn to look at the flowering on the natural rock face by the granite slab. Patches of alyssum, rock roses, tormentil, ground ivy, stonecrop, wild and cultivated plants are growing happily together.

The scent of thyme rises in the still air. My hosts appear. We stay for a moment watching the buzzard glide by, high overhead, then we wander down to the sheltered terrace below the house for a long summer drink. The midges, miraculously, are not on the rampage. Their biting would have been the one thing to drive us indoors. In summer, houses are only for shelter from rain or midge, or for a night's sleep.

We sit quiet, watching a wagtail strut and bob about the turf, happily snatching at whatever insects are near for his supper. We reflect on the amazing balance nature has perfected. The frog, the ladybird, the bee, so many creatures are benefactors in a garden, working away quietly, minding their own business.

'Any hedgehogs about?' I ask.

'Haven't seen one lately, but we're always hoping.'

'M'm . . . So am I.'

'Come and see the new strawberry bed. It's looking promising.'

Strawberries always do well hereabouts. Some years ago a Cornishman grew them by the acre, along with raspberries and daffodils. He has gone but the daffodils survive, to cheer every spring. We wander past the Himalayan poppies, the Peruvian lilies, yellow loosestrife and blue geranium, which I recognise as old friends from my border, to a path of bark chippings, edged by the most glorious massed deep pink dianthus.

'You grew them from seed?'

'I did.'

A quiet smile of satisfaction is allowed, for the nursing of plants such as these does give one a sense of satisfaction. In the border flowers of all kinds grow happily together—sea-holly, soapwort, goldenrod, Jacob's ladder, along with corn marigolds, poppies, corncockle, cranesbill and many more. My friends are keen collectors, always with eyes open for attractive plants. It's good that we have several growing gardens in the neighbourhood now, so that much exchanging of ideas and plants can go on. They are all tended by busy people with limited gardening time. This means they are all the more dearly cherished.

We ignore one another's weeds. Nettles make marvellous soup, we remind any critical strangers, and they are a haven for butterflies. Dandelions bring out the bees and the roots make a very acceptable substitute for coffee. The strangers listen, in half-belief. We reach the strawberry bed. This has been newly made on a patch of field previously sown to a small crop of corn, so it is well manured and protected by a deer fence. The plants look vigorous and happy. There should be much succulent fruit next year.

'The vegetables are doing quite well this year. We'll lead the way.'

I follow on, past the terrace again, to a sheltered corner near the ravine. Vegetables? I can't see any. My host bends down, pulls out and holds up for inspection the most beautiful carrot, clean, straight, tapered to perfection. I look down. There, among an almost jungle-like proliferation of weeds— chickweed, shepherd's purse, sorrel—are rows of superb carrots, beet, swedes, onions—and beyond, holding their heads high or hidden, Brussels sprouts, cauliflower, broccoli, cabbage.

'Good ground-cover!' says my host, a touch ruefully, gouging out a huge handful of chickweed. 'The root crops we can store, but the greens will need more protection before the winter.'

'You mean . . . ?'

'From the four-footed ones'.

'Oh, of course.'

I gaze into the ravine. The water foams white as it falls into smooth, dark pools. The giant oaks overhang it with mystery. Druids must have been here. Today otters travel up this way to the hill-loch, fox and pine marten have their territories mapped. None of these would threaten crops. But this is a garden where a roe-deer may appear at the window in early morning, having breakfasted off lettuce or spinach.

It's a garden after my own heart, full of sap and vigour, a haven for wild plants as well as wild creatures, with hidden corners and sudden, unex-pected flowerings of shrubs and trees—lilac, bird cherry, rowan . . .

I walk home slowly, breathing in the cool, dusk air. A few late swallows are flying high, forecasting another bright day.

July 26th

There are strange cars around these days. Tents appear in odd corners. Occasionally a caravan ventures up. This is the holiday month, of course. This morning I am not surprised to see two people, unknown to me, walk-ing up from the garden gate. They are not young, they are walking slowly, stopping now and again to look round, this way and that. I wait on the doorstep till they come close, then hold out a hand in greeting. They are brother and sister, they tell me, James and Peggy to name. They were at school here fifty-odd years ago.

'We wouldn't have been walking so slowly in those days! My, how those trees have grown', James says, gazing up at the cypresses. 'And the hedge.'

'I remember there were bushes right up to the door,' Peggy says, turning to look back.

'Bushes? . . .'

'Yes. Laurel, I think. Or rhododendron. I'm not sure.'

'And there was a big tree. Too near the house, I thought it was.' James is looking round.

'That must be the stump there.' I point it out.

'That will be it,' he agrees. 'You have a nice green now. When we were at school the war was on and the grass was dug to grow tatties. We all did a lot of work in the garden.'

'And I remember we had to come in the summer holidays to weed the carrots and the peas,' Peggy says, laughing.

'Aye. I remember that all right. But we got some to eat sometimes. That was good. We were always hungry.'

'Were you a big family?'

'No, just the two of us. But we were boarded with a big family. Four of them and two of us, that took some feeding.'

'I'm sure it did. Come on up the garden now.'

They follow me slowly. Clearly their minds are full of memories. What will they make of the enormous compost-heap, the stands of willowherb and sweet cecily? Such things wouldn't have been allowed in their day. They make no comments. Nearing the top of the garden James turns, his face grown young with the glint of his smile.

'I see the old apple-tree is still standing. I remember . . .'

'Aye. And I remember the sore stomachs we had, eating yon green apples!'

Peggy's smile is wry with memory.

'Come this way,' I say. 'Here's something sweeter.' I pick a huge strawberry for each of them.

'My! That's good. I wish we'd had some of them long ago.'

'We'll have some more when you're ready.'

I take them to see the old schoolrooms. They are quite overcome with memories. Peggy disappears into the 'infants' room'.

'It's still there', she calls in disbelief.

'What, Peggy?'

'The hole in the floorboard where I dropped my slate-pencil. Come and see.'

Sure enough, there is a hole in the floor, in the corner, by the window.

'My! What a row I got! I can feel it yet.'

We laugh. Memories are strange things, sometimes so precise, sometimes misleading. Every summer people come, looking about them with bemused expressions, remembering this, forgetting that, sometimes contradicting each other when memories don't coincide. Their coming is always welcome. So much has changed since they were young here, yet they still see what they want to see—the green apples, the hole in the floorboard, the patch of blaeberries on the roadside bank, the hollow on the hill-side where they fetched sand for scrubbing the kitchen table, the short-cut through the wood that took them down to the grocer's van on a Saturday night. All these memories make the place live for us who are here now.

I settle James and Peggy in chairs on the green. Between us we devour a huge bowl of strawberries, with sugar and cream. I make tea and offer oatcakes and crowdie. They eat with great delight, savouring each mouthful. The noon sun shines on their faces and hands. The meadow-scent rises from the warmed grass. Suddenly a curlew swings into the air, above the moorland opposite. Peggy gasps, stifling a cry.

'A curlew . . . oh, I'm sorry, it makes me . . .'

'Now, now, Peggy. You're O.K.'

She recovers at once. James looks at me in apology.

'It's so . . . bonny . . . here. She . . .'

'Don't worry. I know how she feels. Have you . . . a garden at home?'

'A garden? No. We're in . . . Dundee. That's where we came from.'

Peggy looks up.

'We have . . . a wee back court. I wonder . . . could I . . . take a wee cutting, maybe, for a pot?'

'Of course. What would you like?'

'Well, I could smell it when we came down from the garden. In among the rocks there. It minds me of walking in summer, in our bare feet, along the road to Corro . . .'

'I know. You mean thyme!'

'Aye. That's it.'

'Of course you shall have some. I've walked that Corro road . . .'

I dig up a plant for her, carefully, and ease it into a pot. She smiles her thanks, keeping her smile bravely. I often wonder how that little thyme is doing in the wee back court. I'm sure I shall hear one day.

AUGUST

August 2nd

A good summer day and I commit the unforgivable sin of setting off for a two-week spell, leaving the garden on its own. Kind neighbours will check that the gates are kept shut against wandering sheep. The roe deer are well up the hill at this time. But rabbits are reappearing perilously near and a pair of pheasants go scuttering over the wall when I go up to collect some strawberries. One year I found a whole family of them in the long grass under the apple trees. The cat will be on patrol, of course, and I've seen her catch a young hare as big as herself. Young hares, poor souls, are rather stupid and tend to lie crouched too long, imagining themselves invisible. Then their legs are still clumsy and can't match the speed of a practised feline.

So . . . I'm off to the station in a kind friend's car. There's time for a browse at the bookstall and to indulge in buying one of the glossiest of gardening magazines. Gardening colour photography has now reached such a peak of quality that the images one gazes at seem totally unreal. Could one really have a herb garden where the plants grow to such perfection, in rows interspersed with neat box hedges and weedless paths? Could cabbage, cauliflower, carrot, beet reach such sublime form as to appear almost too good to eat? I sigh involuntarily, thinking of my garden on the rampage, weeds choking nascent late sowings, predators lurking in every corner and emerging undeterred. Then I close the glossy pages and gaze at the changing scene outside the carriage window.

Leaving the hill spaces and the wooded glens the train passes through one set of suburbs after another. I glimpse small patches of garden, a shed here, a greenhouse there, a row of begonia, a bed of roses, and imagine the pleasure these small plots must give. But I'm thankful for my own old flowering wilderness and begin to think about taking the first train back to it. Sense prevails, however, and I disembark at Glasgow, my stopover for a few days.

Next morning my first call is to the Botanic Gardens. A deep breath of grass-scented air and a chat with friendly gardeners and the chaos of the streets is distanced. The great glass-houses with their displays of exotic plants are really not for me, but I find quite fascinating a bed showing the dates, back to the sixteenth century, when various flowers were introduced to this country.

"you have orchids growing in the yard!"

Glasgow, the 'dear, green place', has many little unexpected oases of greenery. A patch of grass, some flowering shrubs, a seat where, perhaps, a house had stood. Even the derelict buildings sprout ferns and happy looking buddleias. The gardens of Kelvingrove, with the river running through, the pond, the glorious trees and the grass and the huge herbaceous borders make a place to spend at least one summer's day.

August 7th

Today brings the start of the second part of my holiday. A bus journey from Glasgow to the West, to the coast of Kintyre, and a brief ferry crossing to the small green island of Gigha. Here I enjoy hospitality in a building which once housed a school and part of which is now a post office. It proves to be a home from home. In Gigha, Sir James Horlick, fifty years ago, created the famous Achamore (Big Field) Gardens, to which I make instant pilgrimage. His greatest passion was for rhododendrons. These and other flowering shrubs are, of course, best seen in spring, when people from all over the world come to visit. Thanks to the drift of the Gulf Stream and the shelter of mature trees many plants of all kinds grow happily here.

Once again shunning the exotica, I linger in the walled gardens and take shelter from the rain, with a friendly tabby, in a little old greenhouse. When the sky clears I climb up to the viewpoint, where the hills of Islay and Jura and even the coastline of Ireland stand out miraculously blue across the blue water. A memorable moment!

Back down the steeply winding path, where I hear busy bees foraging, I explore the named parts of the gardens—the Hospital Garden, not, as I first thought, a place for growing medicinal herbs, but a place where sickly plants are cared for, in the shelter of cypress hedges; the Fragrant Garden, which explains itself; Hugh's Border (who was Hugh?); and the Malcolm Allen garden, named after the Head Gardener who worked here for fifty years. These are gardens which have to be visited many times.

Feeling almost overwhelmed with the sight and the scent of so many plantings, I wander back to my pleasant lodging. All along the roadside and the bordering fields nature has done her own sowing. Meadowsweet and purple loosestrife grow in profusion everywhere, beyond hedges of fuchsia and little white and pink roses. The delicate forms of harebell and yellow bedstraw edge the roadside banks. Corn marigolds brighten the fields of barley and oats.

Visitors from the towns and from country places that are drenched in chemicals can only marvel at this flowering. And here we have the late summer picture. Early summer is the time to come, when the machair is carpeted with primroses, gentian, thyme, flowers of every form and colour. It's good that such places are holding their own and producing a valuable surplus to boot. Big herds of dairy cattle and goats mean a daily export of milk to the mainland and cheeses which go all over the world.

Gigha . . . the name, they say, means 'God's Island'. I think God keeps an eye on all these islands in the west. Let's hope they can continue as part of the first patterning of things.

August 14th

With eyes fresh from looking at long distances of sea and far-off hill, I walk up my old garden again. Weeds, weeds, weeds, of course, have been having things their own way. However much you try to accept that they are to be lived with, sometimes you wish they were a little less exuberant. Chickweed and shepherd's purse among the salad crops are easily pulled out, but those wretched old horse-tails have been invading the herbs again. There are still late strawberries and raspberries. The peas, both plain and mangetout, are standing proud, all weeds well smothered, pods shining with health.

I gather the makings of a good summer surplus of salad and fruit, then, before reckoning up the jobs that must be done, take a wander round the flowers. The willowherb is full of the sound of foraging bees. The annuals, always late in developing here, are putting on their show for me—cornflowers of every colour that only they can produce, scarlet flax, marigold. In the wildflower corner, to my delight, corn marigolds and scabious are out. The robin gives me a short burst of song—a lovely sound, but with a tinge of sadness, for it signifies the turning of the year. Butterflies are everywhere still—white cabbage, tortoiseshell, Scotch argus, small blue—and moths which I can't put a name to. It's good to be back with my familiars.

Ripe apples will not fall about my head this year, nor will I stumble on one of Andrew Marvell's lovely melons, though I did once grow a passable pumpkin on a compost heap. There are no plums to speak of, either. These two harvests will be sadly missed. Many a succulent pudding, many a jar of jam or jelly will just not be there. The early summer frost and snow must be the cause of the dearth. No doubt next year the trees will produce a bounty, after a season's retreat.

Reaching the top of the garden I look up. Something else is missing. The rowans are green-leaved and fresh, but there is no shine of scarlet berries.

No rowan jelly, no rowan wine? It's unthinkable. I'll have to forage further afield, perhaps on the lower ground. I remember last year, when the boughs were weighted to the ground with fruit. The 'snow-birds' will be disappointed when they fly in from the cold.

I, too, feel bereft of this grand blaze of colour and promise of succulence, but there, just over the garden wall, is the flowering we can always depend on—the heather, in great sheets of colour, from pale to deepest purple, the honey-scent of it riding on the light summer wind.

Drawn irresistibly, I leave the garden and follow the old footpath, nearly overgrown now, by the hut circles and clearance mounds, towards the high croft lands. Footpaths through the heather, linking neighbour with neighbour, are rare enough today. Wide access roads to plantations of trees or houses are needed now, for the carrying of wheeled and motorised traffic.

Walking on, I remember what the heather must have meant to our ancient forebears—nourishment, warmth, shelter. It still means sustenance to grouse and bees, but it's not looked after as it was in former times, when planned burning of the old plants meant the subsequent growth of fresh, tasty shoots. I stop to watch my honey bees taking their fill, then wander back, still reluctant to pull out a weed, remove a dead flower head, stake up a rambling plant. The garden has got on quite well without me, I reflect. It has had its own quiet little riot of growing and flowering. Tomorrow will be time enough for some taming, for thinning of carrots, for tying of peas, for gathering of late rasps.

Feeling like the lady of old who had only to 'go down the garden smiling', I stretch out a hand to gather some flowers for a neighbour, some marguerites and yellow larkspur which proliferate. Suddenly, the sight of that hand amazes me. It is smooth and clean, with dazzling white finger nails—a holiday hand! It's high time to get some dirt into those crevices and under those nails, I say, almost aloud, to the bees in the flower heads and a passing butterfly!

August 19th

With the garden spruced up after my holiday desertion I find myself dogged by an almost irresistible longing for a sight of the sea again. Childhood memories may have something to do with it. I can so clearly remember rushing barefoot across firm yellow sand and straight into the water. How can I justify asking a kind friend to take me the short trip by car to the nearest stretch of sea? I have it! We could bring back seaweed for next year's crops! The sky is blue today, there's a slight breeze, so the water will be dazzling. I lift the phone.

'You're right. Seaweed is grand manure. Have you plastic bags?'

'I have.'

'Good. I'll be up at one.'

Agreement is very satisfactory. We stuff bags into the capacious boot and set off happily.

It's not the open sea we are making for, but a firth, a long inlet off the north sea, where wintering geese, ducks and swans find shelter and food and which is often graced by the presence of dolphins. We go round by the head of the firth and emerge onto the road which runs close to the shore. I open the window wide to get a whiff of the salt air. It sets the blood racing!

The tide is out. There is no firm yellow sand here, only stretches of pale mud, but the smell of the seaweed is authentic and irresistible. We draw in to a layby and take a long look. The water out there is a dazzle of blue, with the white flecks of small waves riding in from the east. A pair of swans is riding in, too, with a small flotilla of young ones in their wake. They must have nested happily. There are mallard in good numbers and family groups of shelduck busy feeding at the tide-line. They nest here, too, along the shore. To see the dolphins leap would be asking too much of our luck, but we scan the water carefully, nevertheless. We remember other times, when we've seen these fabulous creatures suddenly emerge, in formation, disappear, then emerge again, as though tantalising us with play. Joyful and carefree as they appear, we know that their existence is a miracle, with all the dangers that lurk in the seas these days.

The upper reaches of this firth are, in fact, mercifully free of pollution, with no heavy shipping penetrating this far. Birds that normally live far out at sea sometimes seek refuge here from storm and starvation. The seaweed is uncontaminated.

We unearth the wellingtons, a couple of heughs and the plastic bags and set out to cut our crop of bladderwrack. It's a pleasant task on such a day and soon accomplished when there are only half a dozen bags to fill.

My thoughts go back to the days of the 'kelping'. In the middle of the eighteenth century it was discovered that the calcinated ash of the seaweed known as 'tangle' was rich in alkali, which was used for bleaching linen, an important crop at the time, and in the manufacture of glass and soap. The burning of the seaweed became an important industry for a time. People were offered the inducement of small, enclosed holdings, known as 'crofts', to supplement their incomes, if they would work at the kelping. This was, in fact, the start of what became known as the 'crofting' system of land-holding, as opposed to the old way of working the ground in 'rigs', or long, unenclosed strips. Many people were attracted by this arrangement and came to work the kelp. It was extremely hard work and led to much suffering—rheumatism and pneumonia brought on by exposure to the cold and wet. After the end of the Napoleonic wars cheaper sources of alkali were imported from Spain and the kelp industry collapsed. Latterly, in some of the islands, Alginate Industries have been reviving the processing of seaweed and it is still used there, of course, for fertilising the fields.

'We could do with a trailer-load of this stuff', I say, coming out of my thoughts.

'We certainly could. Maybe we'll come again another day.'

With this happy mutual assurance we make tracks back to the car. The seaweed will be stacked, for digging in next winter. I'll chop some up to make activator for the compost heaps. If I had more I'd burn some, as the kelpers did, to make a marvellous fertilizing agent. It can also be liquidised and can be used as a mulch. With all this in mind I find that another trip to the beach is essential. This one has been wonderful.

The tide is on the turn now, long, smooth ripples sweeping in towards the shore. Looking up to the tall hills at the head of the firth, feeling the movement of the water and smelling the sun-warmed seaweed, it can seem almost as though we are in the west. The flowers are here too—sea-pink and silverweed and the little white roses. Later on there will be brambles. I hope the water level never rises to drown this lovely shore.

Out there, nearly covered now by the rising tide, is the outline of a crannog, a little man-made island where people once lived in happy retreat from the dangers of the world. They probably ate the seaweed, fresh or dried, as the kelpers did, and as people still do in Wales and in the Far East. I must try a dish of it myself. What's so good for the garden must be good for the gardener, too.

The sky is clouding, the wind rising, with the sting of rain on the cheek. A kelper's day, after all! But we've had the magic of it, too. We travel home happily, determined to return.

August 23rd

The rain is still falling relentlessly. The backlog of jobs is piling high. In theory the wearing of rubber boots and plastic garments should make one impervious to weather conditions, at least in summer. But is this summer? Sometimes one wonders. It becomes a case of watching ceaselessly for a break in the cloud cover, rushing out to finish the task abandoned when the last downpour came along, say, the thinning of the carrots. The late raspberries have perished, sadly, on the stalk. There will be a lack of jam this year. Of course, one can weed in the rain, but the work doesn't prosper. Too much earth is taken up with the roots. As you scrabble about to get done before the next pelting of hailstones or raindrops, the weeds you missed start to thrive maliciously in their new-found, roomy, damp beds.

The old people had a song to help them through every kind of monotonous labour—rowing a boat, harvesting, spinning, churning, milking. The cows became so used to the milking song that they wouldn't let down their milk without it. Waulking the cloth, that is, shrinking it by handling, was a long, monotonous process. A dozen women would gather at one place, sitting in rows along a makeshift table, working the cloth with their hands. The songs they sang were often composed extempore and were mostly satirical, poking fun at menfolk of their acquaintance. This must have been a therapeutic exercise! I feel almost inspired to compose something, something satirical, at least about the weather!

The rain eases, thinning to drizzle. I empty another pailful of weeds onto the compost heap and turn to a more positive job, and one done standing upright—fixing extra stakes for the peas. This is a crop that never fails. The pods swell whatever the weather. Shelling them always reminds me of childhood summers. This was a Saturday morning chore. It's sad that so many of today's children see peas only as something coming out of a can, as they see milk only in a bottle. The discarded pods always made a delicacy for Bridget the goat. Nowadays I give them to my neighbour for her chickens. I pick a couple of pods of mange-tout for instant consumption. They're best eaten raw.

The beans, too, are looking sturdy. They'll provide many a good supper dish, with a thick cheese sauce and some salad. Absorbed in the task of staking and indulging in memories, I suddenly realise that no moisture is falling from above. I look up. Unbelievably, the sky has cleared to a pale greenish yellow in the west. A watery sky, this, but at least something is trying to shine, somewhere. Positive thoughts come thronging in, thoughts about the future. It's always next year in a garden and soon it will be planting time, planting for next year. Then I remember—I have a garden centre token, a present from those who understand my way of living.

The nearest garden centre in the town is a vast emporium. I most often feel as bewildered and disoriented there as I do in one of the bigger supermarkets. That seemingly endless array of seed packets, from all the different merchants, the flowers so temptingly depicted, dazzles the mind. I know I shall succumb to their appeal, though sense tries to tell me they'll never succeed in my small battered plots. Bulbs are a better proposition. Most of them survive and flourish here, though a few fall foul of that old pheasant's beak. I'll probably opt for small, low-growing things—crocus (for the bees), dwarf iris, snowdrops, aconite.

Different brands of fertilizer and weed-killer take up what seems like acres of space. Sometimes I shudder at the thought of all those chemicals being scattered over so many gardens everywhere. They may help in the production of cabbages like footballs, carrots as thick as your arm and some dazzling blooms fit for the flower show. But . . . I close my eyes and think of the island machair—those little tight crops of barley, corn marigolds happily flowering among it, tiny wild pansies bordering the bounds . . . Seaweed is what the ground loves here. There are loads and loads of it to hand.

For a time, two hundred years ago, when the lairds found there was money to be made in burning the seaweed to produce kelp, the crofters were forbidden to use it as manure. Now they are being actively encouraged to ignore 'artificials' and go back to the old methods. The thought of those few faraway acres being tended as they should be is an inspiration which helps in periods of despondency and gloom when reminders rush in, reminders of the damage being done to this lovely planet of ours.

So I shall turn away from the displays of chemical products to gaze incredulously at the rows of garden machinery—strimmers, angled hedge-trimmers, shiny spades, two-way hoes. And lawn-mowers almost the size of a small car. Anything powered would be sure to break down with me. I shall choose my bulbs and opt for a useful-looking gadget—a hand-held device for planting bulbs in wild places, for naturalising, under trees. Then I shall wander round the outside section, looking quite longingly at flowering shrubs priced a long way out of my reach, consoling myself with the thought that they probably wouldn't like the move anyway, repair to the café for a hot drink and come home loaded with catalogues to browse through and discard.

August 28th

I'm up early today, for a check on the weather. It looks promising—puffs of high white cloud with sheets of blue between. I scan the whole spectrum, hoping the magic will hold. I'm almost sure it will. I can remember only very few wet days for the Games. This is Games Day in the glen. People come, now, from many parts to compete and to watch. In years gone by it was a time, between harvesting the hay and cutting the corn, when folk could meet, engage in feats of skill and endurance, sing, dance, exchange greetings and news. It's still like that, though a certain element of entertainment and perhaps of over-competitiveness has crept in.

In the morning, heats are run off for the various races. By early afternoon the crowds are arriving. From all over the world they come, tourists and holiday-makers, some wearing exotic clothing, speaking in excited, unrecognisable tongues. There is track racing, high and long jumping, a cycle race, then the entry of exhausted marathon runners from the town.

Some of the special things go almost unnoticed—small girls in their beautiful Highland garb, dancing their hearts out on a tiny platform; young men, in quiet corners, playing pibroch to a steady tread in front of the judges' shelter.

Time goes quickly as friends meet friends not seen since the last Games. Wise people take a picnic snack to share, as the tea-tent and the ice-cream stall always sport queues. There's talk, inevitably, of the weather over the year, of sheep and cattle prices, of 'set-aside' and much speculation about what the government may be up to next. Fatalism usually surfaces and there's always time for a good joke and a laugh, as the men toss back a nip from a proferred bottle. The Games are to be celebrated, come what may!

The pipe band marches by, players resplendent in kilt and bonnet, giving a mighty lift to the occasion. Then we settle to watching the 'real' events of the day. We scan the nearby hill-side for a sight of the hill-race runners as they emerge above the tree-line, a gap showing, now, between the fast and the slow. With glasses and telescopes we watch the progress of the pack. This race recalls the time when news had to be carried by runners from glen to glen, by hill tracks, in every kind of weather.

The 'heavy' events have their origins in everyday doings of former times. 'Tossing the caber' is a feat demanding unimaginable strength and skill, when something like a telegraph pole has to be lifted and flung so that it goes up and over in as straight a line as possible. This, at one time, was found to be a way of getting felled trees clear of the wood, when they were needed for building or other purposes.

Weight-throwing was said to be a pastime enjoyed by men waiting at the blacksmith's for jobs to be completed at the anvil. Testing your skill and strength against another's has always been attractive to the young.

The hill-runners come back to the arena with applause for each one of them. The winner looks almost as fresh as when he set out, the tailenders are almost at the point of exhaustion, but they come in, one and all. Modern living has not ruined as many constitutions as was feared.

At last the final event of the day looms large—the tug-o'-war. This is when the 'heavies' really show their worth. Muscles bulge, chests heave, as the opposing teams dig in their heels and amass their will-power. Spectators suffer with them as they egg on their favoured side. When the final collapse comes there is much good humour and hand-shakes as winners and losers take their leave.

After long applause people begin to disperse, slowly, happily. There's the nostalgic sound of old fairground music, the smell of chips and hot doughnuts. The children have a last go on the 'dodgems', a last lick of iced-lollies and it's home, five, ten, twenty, fifty miles away or more, maybe to some lonely place in the hills, where gatherings such as today's are highly prized.

'It was a good Games,' one friend says. 'The best,' says another. 'See you next year,' says a third. I smile in agreement to them all. Then it's back to 'auld claes and parritch'. The garden has had peace without me. I'll be back there on Monday, tearing out weeds, cutting back bushes, digging out compost, with renewed energy and drive.

SEPTEMBER

September 2nd

One glorious day this week raised hopes of an Indian summer. It was not to be. Nevertheless for eight beautiful hours the sun, our old 'hay-maker', dazzled us from a sky of ultramarine, as if to reassure us that he is still hereabouts. We stretched out on the grass—skin troubles, headaches, the very thought of them dismissed, as we revelled in the luxury of a brief spell of heat.

Now we are back to reality, with grey skies, a north wind, misty mornings and drizzle. Misty mornings can give moments of sheer delight, when the sun breaks through to light up the thousands of delicate cobwebs linking the wayside grasses and flowers. Perhaps one of those mornings is still to come.

Meantime it's a question of sorting out priorities in the line of jobs. I heard somewhere that 'good gardeners garden in the autumn'. Inspired by this timely thought I set out to work. It certainly is autumn. The birches on the hill over the road are slowly changing colour. Leaves from the garden rowans crinkle against my face, as the soft wind comes from the west.

It's difficult, this year, to accept the fact that summer has gone, for it seems as though it never really came. Yet things have grown. Some have outgrown their strength, grown sappy. Indeed, over the last two or three years everything seems to have had an explosion of growth. Trees, the birches and rowans, the hawthorn hedge, weeds, of course, all seem to have grown greatly taller, as though they were groping for the sun. Foxgloves, six feet high, stand sentinel above the garden wall. Whether this is part of global warming or not, people disagree. The facts remain. I read of a farmer in Aberdeenshire who cropped a field of sunflowers, though he counted only four days of sun. He harvested them for the oil, and florists, he said, had customers avid for the flower heads. I remember, nostalgically, the fields in Slovakia. We spent a memorable holiday, once, in Slovakia. There, in vast fields, the sunflowers stand, turning their heads, majestically, to the sun. '*Tourne-sol*' the French call them. Perhaps I could try some, next year . . . ?

Autumn is the time for planning. I make a start at re-shaping the bed below the sitting-room window. The clematis I planted two years ago, and had almost given up for dead, is thrusting nicely up into the ivy in the corner by the porch. I decide to cut back other climbers, put in more spring bulbs—crocus, scylla, miniature iris—and low-growing plants—thyme, alyssum, aubretia, campanula, all well-loved flowers with manageable roots.

It's good to get the spade into the ground again and to be planning and planting. When work has to stop for a heavy shower I plant the indoor bulbs—hyacinths and crocuses, yellow ones to bring sunlight a little nearer in the dark days. A neighbour has a most attractive rock garden, with limited space and exuberant plantings, so that I am lucky enough to be able to offer a home to plants clamouring for *lebensraum*.

In my turn I look for homes in the burgeoning gardens of new residents for my exuberant growths of blue geraniums, larkspur, marguerites, Peruvian lilies, herbs of all kinds, which were given to me when I started planting. Two days of scrabbling about among the plants, clearing weeds and stones, and my hands are recognisable again. I never feel happy in gloves, except for gathering nettles or pruning roses.

The flower border under the west wall needs a drastic cutting back. Every year I say this and every year I do give away boxes of roots, yet every year there's overcrowding. Perhaps the plants are too well sheltered, when they spread so happily. The deep pink flowers of astrantia have been thrusting through the orange Peruvian lilies, making their own most attractive colour patterning. Now, with autumn, Michaelmas daisies are everywhere. The real signal of the turning of the year is the flowering of montbretia. For most of the summer it keeps itself to itself, but then it makes a real show—though a slightly sad one, the last till next year.

Going in to supper as the light begins to fade, I notice honey fungus on the logs edging the small raised beds beside the holly tree. I'm glad it has its brief spell of growth, for it has a strange beauty, though it flourishes in decay.

That evening I hear a light thudding against the uncurtained window, where the moths flit. Bats are on the move! A cheering thought, when so much wildlife is in peril.

September 14th

Wildlife of a more terrestrial kind is on the move today. I had heard that rabbits were reappearing not far away. Now one is lolloping happily across the green. Frowning almost in the style of Mr McGregor in the Beatrix Potter story, I watch from the window. I remember bygone days when each small cabbage plant had to grow in the protection of a plastic jar. Cloches were expensive and could be burrowed under or overturned in a gale. Will these days come back? I scrutinise the esculents. No damage is apparent yet. I think of people with gardens almost impossible to fence who had to give up growing everything but root crops on account of rabbits, hares or roe deer. Hares and the very occasional roe I have here, but rabbits . . . ! I come, momentarily, to a full stop.

Root crops have been meagre this year, carrots poorly, though I grew marigolds and spring onions for protection. Beetroot, which I depend on for winter salads, is also very sketchy. Only summer turnips are really plentiful. The onions are reasonably sound, if on the small side. It's good to see, and smell, them, lifted and drying in the sun and wind.

With a few square yards of bare ground visible, at last I settle to some autumn digging. Has anyone, I sometimes wonder, got ground like mine, with wriggles of old tree-roots, rogue raspberry shoots, never-ending stones? Pictures from those glossy, and even not so glossy, gardening magazines flash through the mind. I think of the television programmes watched avidly and, it must be admitted, enviously. Other people's ground always appears so smooth and clean, almost in its pristine state. Perhaps such perfection might pall. There is certainly great satisfaction in actually clearing a piece of ground, making it ready to receive seed or seedling.

Forgetting rabbits, their staggering rate of increase and the havoc they threaten for next spring, I take a weekend walk up the road. Panacea can always be found somewhere there!

A Highland autumn has a special, fragile feel. Spring is often disappointing, late, long-awaited and chilling. Autumn lingers precariously, as though reluctant to give in. There is usually a fresh green bite for sheep and cattle till well into November.

This day the roadside is bright with late summer flowering. Scabious! There should be a colour known as scabious, for it's a shade of blue of its own amazing intensity. Thistles of all sizes, yarrow, tansy, add their special forms and colours. Further up, where large loads of earth had been dumped as in-fill at a widening point, bright yellow mustard has shot up, above a covering of delicate fumitory. Further on again, deep ditching had been done and here, incredibly, patches of red poppies and ox-eye daisies have appeared. Red poppies have not been seen for years. The seed, I believe, can stay in the ground for long periods and the plants emerge when conditions are right.

So these are colourful days indeed. Soon, as the heather fades, the bracken will be turning gold and brown. The only colour sadly lacking is that brilliant red of the rowan berries. I must take time for a walk down to the low ground. The hazel nuts look promising. I had a Swedish friend who would gather them green, for pickling. I tend to wait till they're on the ground. The brambles are still hardly out of the flowering stage, so that's another harvest which must wait. I gather three big brown boletus from the roadside and wander home for tea.

House martens are darting and swooping in the high air, gearing up for that incredible journey to their winter quarters. We shall miss them.

Back in the garden I try to take a long detached look, to see the prospect as a whole. It is, after all, only a portion taken from the wild, from the heather and scrub, from self-sown conifers and birches. The wild would so gladly take it back and let its native creatures have their fill. Even now parts of it are developing a will of their own, and in a way of singular beauty. That willowherb, those grasses, ferns and ground-ivy in the wall, mosses on the stones, who could devise anything so innately appropriate? I think of the advocates of Permaculture, who favour letting things grow in harmony and find living space happily together. Not for me trim lawns, neat parterres, knot gardens or topiary. I found a somewhat disappointing passage in Vita Sackville-West's *The Garden Book*:

> Then there are dead-nettles. You have to be a very highbrow gardener indeed to like dead-nettles. Personally I prefer every nettle of every kind dead and eradicated, but then I must confess to a preference for keeping my garden weedless and tidy.

Perhaps she never knew the taste of nettle soup! Feeling suddenly hungry at the thought, I put a fork to the first of the year's potatoes. The tubers come up dry and clean. New-dug potatoes for supper, with eggs, a dish of peas and a green salad! That's something the ancient inhabitants of this ground never had. There's a lot to be said for a certain amount of draining, digging, weeding, all that cultivation involves. But the wild growth must have its say.

Some years ago, when I started the reclamation work, I kept half a dozen chickens and a goat. Supper for Bridget, the goat, consisted of a huge armful of nettles, dockens, willow-herb, chickweed, ground ivy, almost any weed available. And she produced a quota of creamy milk after a breakfast of concentrates in the morning. The chickens, too, gave a surplus of huge brown eggs, though the extent of their original free range sometimes meant precious seed was scratched up and they had eventually to be confined to their own corner, with large amounts of green stuff thrown over their fence.

I kept white doves, with a dovecote made from scraps of wood and slate by a neighbour. They roosted mostly on the high rhones of the house. It was a great joy to have them flying down to a call in the morning, their wings translucent in the early sun. They nested and had young, but there was no

105

way of protecting them from the hungry sparrow-hawks which haunted the plantation up the road. Risking their lives daily, the doves gave us many hours of delight. They were greatly missed.

So there it is—a garden on the wild side, a garden which must co-exist with all the forms of life surrounding it, a garden which has taught its gardener many things. There is much to marvel at—a plant thrusting through the smallest gap between heavy stone slabs and producing the most exquisite flower; delicate ferns with roots in the heart of a tree-stump or a dry-stone wall; wild orchids. As one visitor exclaimed, 'you have orchids growing in the yard!'

The introduced food crops may vary in yield from year to year. This autumn the failure of the beetroot is sad and spinach and broccoli have bolted. There's a lesson in that. They should have, and could have, had food and water at appropriate times. Natural growth will seldom fail. It's thanks largely to it—willowherb, heather and many roadside flowers—that the bees are now well and active and may have made some surplus. I'm waiting till the last flowers fade before opening the hive.

September 24th

This is a time to gather seeded heads—of astrantia, of poppies, both oriental and glamorous. Those wonderful deep shades of brown mean mellow fruitfulness just as do ripe plums and apples. I'm not a flower-arranger. Any flowers I gather go straight into a big jug and arrange themselves. But a few dried leaves or flowers will last all winter and foretell seed-time again.

There is still some late flowering about. At this height annuals always bide their time. Nasturtiums are only now making signals, and welcome they are. Michaelmas daisies, of course, keep time with their namesake, he of the flaming sword. Their range of colour is as beautiful as any, fending off winter valiantly. I believe Gertrude Jekyll had a whole border given over to them. And there's a succulence in the tiny Alpine strawberries, which will fruit till the first hard frosts. They have seeded everywhere since I first sowed them years ago. So the garden dies graciously, being certain of rebirth.

Warmed by this feeling of faith in the future which contact with the garden gives, I decide to take one more wander abroad before the impending equinoctial gales, floods, storms of any kind. I take a track through woodlands a few miles from home, a wide track, made for the planting and ultimate extraction of timber. The conifers grow gloomily together. There is little sign of bird or animal life. A few flowers grow limply along the edge of the plantations. A disused double track, probably now serving as a fire-break, takes off through the trees. I follow it, clambering over wind-blown branches, skirting boggy holes. This was once a cart-track through croft land. Among the conifers, on higher ground, to the left, are the tumbled walls of small houses and steadings. To the right is a small glade, grass still growing lush and bright, holding its own, where once there would have been small harvests of oats and hay. Here and there a native tree shines in the gloom, a silver birch, a rowan, a gean. The conifers are sadly dull.

With a sense of relief I reach the higher ground, above the tree-line and on to the open slopes. Here, unbelievably, a late lark is startled into song. Small paths go snaking through the heather, linking the vanished settlements. Neighbours would have walked them many times, carrying news, a bottle of milk from a freshly calved cow, a broody hen to sit on a clutch of eggs, happy exchanges of many kinds.

The wide sky, the glimpses of far-off hills and lochs, would have inspired many a young mind to go travelling, exploring. Some of the greatest plant-hunters must have been born in places like this. China, India, South America took them away, as sailors, missionaries, traders. They would have found ways and means of bringing home pocketfuls of seeds, dried plants, plants in pigs' bladders. I like to think my Peruvian lilies came from a Highland horseman's saddle-bag and thence to his native heath. They grow naturalised in many places hereabouts.

Plants introduced like this found their way mostly into the gardens of big estates, which were modelled on those of the south. Working crofters and farmers had little time to make gardens, though the women grew kale and carrots and herbs for the broth-pot. Wayside flowers were plentiful and fields were bright with poppies, cornflowers and marigolds. Daffodils began to appear at one time, probably in imitation of the garden at the Big House. Now, even at the sites of long-deserted croft-houses, they flourish and spread, undeterred by the attentions of sheep, rabbits, hares, roes or other inquisitive predators.

Where it was possible to fence a small plot round the house and to provide shelter with a hedge of hawthorn or broom, then little pink roses would climb the walls and pansies and forget-me-nots grew happily by the door. Foxgloves would seed and spread, giving height, and, if there was a green for the washing, where the children could play, it would soon become a meadow, full of native flowers of every kind. So a Highland garden was just a small part of the surrounding wild.

Whoever comes after me to this garden will make many changes, I'm sure. Many are needed. Trees have grown too big, making too much shade, and will have to be felled. The hawthorn hedge, which shelters many birds in winter, is trespassing, protruding over the road, where large vehicles

It will always be June

brush against it noisily. Several hidden corners, deep in dead leaves, where I always hoped the hedgehog would settle, will probably have to be cleared. The gigantic compost heap, where rogue potatoes flourish and where nettles and comfrey, cut down in autumn, produce a natural store of plant food, is a legacy of a kind.

A garden is so much more than a piece of ground growing things to order. I remember clearly, as a child of nine, looking in amazement at the tiny plants which had sprung, almost overnight, from the packet of 'cottage garden' seeds I had bought with my pocket money. I came in late for tea, fingers caked in earth after weeding my tiny plot meticulously, with a firm determination to be a gardener. Later, I still considered this seriously, but felt I hadn't enough background in science to become a professional. I've had the good fortune to be always a happy amateur and to have had somewhere, just outside the door, to wander or to work in. Days of stress, sadness or disappointment in any facet of life can be smoothed out as you look at the perfect structure of a flower. You stop and remember that root, stem and leaf have survived frost, snow, gale, every kind of storm or weather. You walk on, gather a sun-warmed strawberry, and realise that growing things give and give.

After this garden? I can think of no other. Indoor plants don't do well for me. I shall have to rely on memory. This store is well-stocked already and capable of total, or almost total, recall. There are few, very few, black spots—the decimation of greens by rabbits or caterpillars, the uprooting of bulbs by the neighbourhood pheasant, a late frost—these will soon be obliterated. All the other images will have the freshness and colour of a morning in June. The scents and sound, too—clover in the early sun, the cuckoo calling from the hill-side birches, the swish of swallows' wings round and round the eaves. It will always be June.